Excellence in Online Journalism

Excellence in Online Journalism

Exploring Current Practices in an Evolving Environment

David A. Craig
University of Oklahoma

Los Angeles | London | New Delhi
Singapore | Washington DC

For information:

SAGE Publications, Inc.
2455 Teller Road
Thousand Oaks,
 California 91320
E-mail: order@sagepub.com

SAGE Publications India Pvt. Ltd.
B 1/I 1 Mohan Cooperative
 Industrial Area
Mathura Road, New Delhi 110 044
India

SAGE Publications Ltd.
1 Oliver's Yard
55 City Road
London EC1Y 1SP
United Kingdom

SAGE Publications Asia-Pacific
 Pte. Ltd.
33 Pekin Street #02-01
Far East Square
Singapore 048763

Printed in the United States of America

Library of Congress Cataloging-in-Publication Data

Craig, David A.
Excellence in online journalism : exploring current practices in an evolving environment / David A. Craig.
     p. cm.
Includes bibliographical references and index.
ISBN 978-1-4129-7009-9 (pbk.)
    1. Online journalism. I. Title.

PN4784.O62C73 2011
070.4—dc22   2010017399

This book is printed on acid-free paper.

10   11   12   13   14   10   9   8   7   6   5   4   3   2   1

Acquisitions Editor:	Todd Armstrong
Assistant Editor:	Aja Baker
Editorial Assistant:	Nathan Davidson
Production Editor:	Brittany Bauhaus
Copy Editor:	Kim Husband
Typesetter:	C&M Digitals (P) Ltd.
Proofreader:	Victoria Reed-Castro
Indexer:	Diggs Publication Services, Inc.
Cover Designer:	Edgar Abarca
Marketing Manager:	Helen Salmon

Brief Contents

Detailed Contents

Preface

It does not take long to find examples of poorly done online journalism or to find critics eager to point those examples out. But this book is based on the belief that it is more valuable for students preparing for the field to see good examples and to think about what excellent work looks like. Like the technologies that support it, the craft of online journalism is evolving quickly. That makes excellence a moving target. But it is a target rooted in a longer history of high-quality journalism.

This book lets students hear from thoughtful practitioners—more than 30 of them—about what excellence in online journalism looks like and how they are pursuing it despite many challenges such as staffing limits, intense competition, and the complex nature of the medium itself. The book also places the evolution of online journalism in a broader context of how the standards of journalism are changing while maintaining common ground with the best traditions of old media. The work is built on the author's experience past and present interviewing more than 100 online and newspaper journalists about the details of their thinking and their best work.

It is a challenge for instructors in online journalism courses to cover both concepts and technical skills effectively. This book is not a technical manual, and plenty of those are available. It will complement more nuts-and-bolts treatments of online work by showing how professionals think about elements of online journalism and provide specific models of excellence to which students can apply their technical skills. With the maturing of online journalism and instruction in this area, it is likely that courses will continue to become more conceptually sophisticated and that quality expectations for student work will grow. These changes make the book more valuable for the combination of concepts and examples it provides.

Although this book discusses online journalism using an ethical framework, it treats ethics differently from both other online journalism books and most textbooks in media ethics. It does not ignore ethical dilemmas. In fact, boxed features in several chapters look at difficult choices in areas such as use of sensitive archived content, where to draw the line on inflammatory user comments, and how to handle reporting of unconfirmed information. But the book, building on the work of philosopher Alasdair MacIntyre and journalism ethicists Sandra Borden and Edmund Lambeth, takes readers beyond individual dilemmas to show how choices to pursue excellence in specific projects help to reshape the understanding of excellence in journalism more broadly. It provides a rich perspective on the development of excellence in the field and what stands in the way. It will help students view powerful tools like social media and interactive graphics for what they can contribute to the development of excellent journalism, not just their value in isolation.

The book also offers a distinctive perspective on how the choices of individual journalists in their daily work can lead to excellent journalism even in a time of stress in the profession. Unlike many discussions of media ethics, it emphasizes personal qualities, or virtues, not codes or rules. These qualities show themselves in on-the-job profiles of four journalists as they face daily challenges and in discussion across several chapters. This emphasis on personal character is important in the current unstable and rapidly changing environment of journalism.

The author developed this book out of a passion for excellence in journalism built on a career first as a newspaper copy editor, then as a teacher of editing helping prepare students for work in print and online media. This project also draws on nearly 20 years studying ethics in journalism and years of teaching students about journalism ethics across media platforms. The author's desire is to help strengthen the future practice of journalism—with respect for both new and old ideas and for the greater purposes of the practice in society.

❖ ANCILLARIES

An author-hosted companion website provides links to examples of online journalism work discussed in each chapter. It will also point readers to new examples of excellence, providing updated material for classroom discussion. Visit the companion site at **www.sagepub.com/craigstudy.**

Acknowledgments

This project would have been impossible without a great deal of help.

Funding for travel to do the initial interviews came from the John S. and James L. Knight Foundation as part of the Carnegie-Knight Initiative on the Future of Journalism Education. I am grateful for that support and, closer to home, for the time and encouragement provided by Dean Joe Foote of the Gaylord College of Journalism and Mass Communication at the University of Oklahoma. I also could not have completed this project without the excellent help of graduate assistants Erin Sigler and Philip Todd.

I thank the journalists I interviewed for carving out time to talk, e-mail, and provide insights from their experience.

I owe an intellectual debt to Sandra Borden of Western Michigan University for her work relating Alasdair MacIntyre's thinking to journalism and for her comments on early sections of my manuscript. Reaching further back, I thank Edmund Lambeth of the University of Missouri for his insights about MacIntyre, his passion for excellence, and his example of an ethical life.

A number of others helped me shape this project to make it more useful to students and instructors. My colleague at Oklahoma, Julie Jones, offered invaluable perspective. I am also grateful for the feedback from a number of reviewers: Timothy E. Bajkiewicz (University of South Florida), Bernhard Debatin (Ohio University), Eileen Gilligan (SUNY Oswego), Steven D. Koski (College of Saint Elizabeth), Mindy McAdams (University of Florida), Kathy Olson (Lehigh University), Al Tompkins (The Poynter Institute), and Michael Williams (University of Kansas).

Thanks are also due to Todd Armstrong at SAGE for his insight and encouragement at many stages of this project.

Finally, I want to acknowledge the love and support of my wife, Barbara, and my children, Elizabeth and Jonathan. I am greatly blessed.

Introduction

Thoughtful journalists in both old and new media push hard to surpass the minimum standards of the craft and produce work that is worthy of respect. But maintaining high standards is difficult because of the pressures on individual journalists and organizations in an era of economic change and upheaval. In the online world, what excellent journalism means is evolving as the roles of professional journalists and users become increasingly intertwined and as online journalists keep experimenting to find the best ways to tell stories and engage audiences.

Journalists who produce online content labor amid multiple challenges:

- How to maintain standards of fairness, completeness, and accuracy in the face of competition from other news sites and people's expectations that they will get information online immediately.

- How to make the most of the online medium's capacity for depth and breadth in storytelling with limited time and staff, and the challenge of unifying disparate parts of a story including video, audio, photos, graphics, and text.

- How to develop excellent stories that meld the contributions of journalists—or those traditionally defined as journalists—and users.

- How to foster conversation and community through blogs, forums, and social media.

This book focuses on what excellent online journalism looks like in an era of rapid change in the media industry and in communication technology. The discussion draws on interviews with more than

30 writers, editors, and producers in online news organizations and dozens of examples of strong work. The primary goal is to inspire future online journalists to pursue their craft at a high standard of quality and help them identify the challenges that stand in the way. This book will also help media scholars and critics better understand the connection between ethics and excellence and more critically evaluate the work and practices of online journalism.

The focus of the book is on work from four news organizations: msnbc.com, washingtonpost.com, WSJ.com (*Wall Street Journal* Online), and NYTimes.com. These four are among the largest web news organizations in staffing and audience. Their work has been recognized for excellence through awards from journalism organizations such as the Online News Association. Many of the journalists who work for them are experienced in both new and old media, so they bring a valuable perspective on standards and challenges in online journalism.

But the biggest outlets don't have a monopoly on good work, and they are not immune to problems and mistakes. Excellent work in online journalism comes from all sizes of organizations. Some of the best work has flowed from news organizations in midsize cities, small community sites, and independent operations. Profiles of some talented journalists at organizations of several sizes will showcase their good work and the challenges they face.

The discussion in the book builds on foundational interviews with writers, editors, and producers at the four large news organizations in 2007. Follow-ups with a number of these since then, along with new interviews with several talented journalists at large and small operations in 2009 and 2010, provide additional insight on developments in the practice. Examples come from the work of these journalists and others over the last several years—both well-known examples that shaped future thinking in the field and lesser-known ones that highlight elements of excellence.

Chapter 1 lays the groundwork for the rest of the book by looking at the meaning of excellence in journalism and introducing four elements of online excellence: speed and accuracy with depth in breaking news, comprehensiveness in content, open-endedness in story development, and the centrality of conversation. Chapter 2 sets out an ethical model that sheds light on how practices such as journalism evolve or deteriorate. The model is based on the work of philosopher Alasdair MacIntyre and journalism ethicists Sandra Borden and Edmund Lambeth. The chapter lays out a central theme: that the practice of journalism is developing in ways that encompass old challenges and possibilities but also redefine them.

The focus turns in Chapters 3 through 6 to an in-depth look at the four elements of online excellence. These four developing standards provide a framework for better understanding what excellence in online journalism means. Comments from the journalists and insights from the ethical model introduced in Chapter 2 help to clarify how standards of excellence in new media are like the standards of old media but build on them in distinctive ways, what challenges make it difficult to do high-quality work, and what personal qualities are needed to achieve excellence despite them. Each of these chapters includes numerous examples to help make the discussion specific. The work is wide ranging, encompassing breaking news stories, multimedia projects, blogs, forums, and social media. An on-the-job profile at the end of each chapter shows how one online journalist faces daily challenges and juggles responsibilities.

Chapter 7 focuses on excellence in smaller mainstream websites and independent ones including citizen journalism initiatives and independent blogs. Chapter 8 looks to challenges that are likely to continue into the future of online journalism in a complex and changing environment.

1

Excellence Online

A Work in Progress

Journalists take a beating every day for their ethics and their competence. Bloggers on the left and right criticize decisions by mainstream media outlets. Critics on radio and television call into question the fairness of news coverage. Much of the public deeply doubts the trustworthiness of reporters and editors (Kohut et al., 2009).

While bad news and opinions about journalists spread rapidly, good journalists at hundreds of large and small news organizations strive for excellence in the face of growing financial pressures and often shrinking resources.

This chapter will:

- Show how excellence is an important but shifting concept in journalism.

- Introduce four elements of excellence in online journalism based on interviews with journalists. These four elements will be the focus of discussion of online journalists' work in the next several chapters.

❖ EXCELLENCE IN OLD AND NEW MEDIA

It has never been easy to do excellent journalism, but news people and news organizations have been thinking about excellence for a long time. From the early 20th century, the professionalization of journalism brought increasing attention to the value of high standards of quality. The founding of journalism schools such as the University of Missouri highlighted an interest in training future journalists to pursue their craft with greater skill and understanding. The creation of journalism professional organizations such as the Society of Professional Journalists and Women in Communications in 1909 (Gallagher, 1998) started drawing together journalists with an interest in increasing the quality of work in the field. Numerous journalism organizations articulated standards through codes of ethics—among them, in the 1920s, the American Society of Newspaper Editors, the National Association of Broadcasters, and the SPJ (Ferré, 1998). A number of publications critically reviewing journalism appeared in the mid-20th century, including *Nieman Reports* in 1947 and *Columbia Journalism Review* in 1961, and continued in later decades to raise important questions about practices in the field (Bertrand, 1998).

The nature of excellence in journalism is evolving with the development of online journalism. In 2004, looking back at previous research about journalism quality, sociologist and newspaper researcher Leo Bogart wrote:

> American editors and journalists share a fairly broad consensus on what constitutes excellence in the press. When experienced news people are asked what makes for quality, a number of words and phrases inevitably surface: integrity, fairness, balance, accuracy, comprehensiveness, diligence in discovery, authority, breadth of coverage, variety of content, reflection of the entire home community, vivid writing, attractive makeup, packaging or appearance, and easy navigability. In the American tradition, but not always accepted elsewhere, is the clear differentiation of reporting and opinion. (2004, p. 40)

At the core of journalistic excellence is strong reporting and storytelling, as recognized in the field through a variety of awards. For example, the Pulitzer Prizes, first awarded in 1917, have honored powerful investigative pieces and other in-depth reporting, heart-rending feature stories, and gripping photography (The Pulitzer Prizes, n.d.). Other awards such as the Edward R. Murrow Awards of the Radio Television Digital News Association recognize news and feature reporting in broadcast journalism (Awards—Edward R. Murrow Awards, n.d.).

Ideas about excellence online have a lot in common with old media, but some shifts are evident. Three journalism researchers developed a list of excellence criteria with new media in mind (Gladney, Shapiro, & Castaldo, 2007). They included many elements common with print excellence such as good writing, appropriate redesign, depth, and community building/service. But other criteria—such as search power, multimedia richness, bandwidth, and user choice/control—were distinctively online elements. Some others such as community dialogue and "hyperlocal" were particularly important online.

As with journalism in general, ideas about excellence in online work are reflected in awards. For example, the Online News Association's Online Journalism Awards have honored public service, general excellence, breaking news, investigative journalism, multimedia feature presentation, and other categories of work (About the Online Journalism Awards, n.d.). The Knight-Batten Awards for Innovations in Journalism from J-Lab: The Institute for Interactive Journalism highlight creative work including citizen-generated journalism (Knight-Batten Awards for Innovations in Journalism, n.d.).

Thinking about excellence in online journalism continues to develop as technology changes and creative journalists experiment with new ways of communicating—and as the public takes a more central place in storytelling and discussion through tools such as social media. The possibilities emerging for online journalism reshape the broader picture of what journalism can look like and what it can do for the public. The next section will lay out four key elements of excellence in online journalism. They are all evolving, but together they represent the core of the definition of excellence in this book.

❖ EXCELLENCE ONLINE: FOUR DEVELOPING STANDARDS

The journalists interviewed for this book all face a steep challenge: trying to understand what excellence means in a medium that is young and evolving quickly. They can look back to the traditions of the old media, which some of them came from, but their work is situated in an environment that is different economically, technologically, and socially. Hal Straus, interactivity and communities editor at washingtonpost.com, pointed back to common ground with the tradition of print journalism:

> I don't think there's any fundamental difference between excellence in online journalism and excellence in print journalism. You have to be

able to present information and commentary on issues that matter to your audience in a thorough and provocative way. The facts have to be right, your opinions have to be well argued and supported, and so there has to be a recognition that most issues have more than one side.

As Straus noted, the tradition of journalism is to provide people reliable information about important public matters, as well as opinions on these topics. Online journalists still strive to do this—the best ones, with great care. But he and other online journalists also point to ways that online excellence looks distinctive and carries its own distinctive challenges.

This section will introduce four elements of excellence that will be the focus of discussion in much of this book: speed and accuracy with depth in breaking news, comprehensiveness in content, open-endedness in story development, and centrality of conversation. (See Table 1.1 for a summary.) These stood out from interviews with writers, editors, and producers. They overlap with issues from old media, but they are particularly important in online journalism and have a distinct character in this medium. Together they provide a framework for thinking more carefully about online excellence.

Table 1.1   Developing Standards of Excellence in Online Journalism

Speed and accuracy with depth in breaking news	• Making the most of the Internet's capacity for speed while taking care to confirm the accuracy of information and disclose exactly what is known, and how, for any information that is not confirmed • Providing context and background quickly
Comprehensiveness in content	• Using multiple storytelling forms—text, graphics, audio, photos, video—in ways that take greatest advantage of their individual strengths and the sum of the parts
Open-endedness in story development	• Developing stories in multiple stages in line with their appropriate life spans, drawing on contributions from the public with both respect and careful judgment
The centrality of conversation	• Fostering interaction with and among users through means including distinctive voice and personality, direct address, balancing monitoring and self-direction in discussions, and establishing a wide presence through social media

Speed and Accuracy With Depth in Breaking News: Chapter 3

As a medium, the Internet provides the means to break stories at any time and update news continually. But the best of online journalism balances speed with other considerations such as context and thoroughness. Accuracy remains a top priority.

Jim Roberts, associate managing editor for digital news at NYTimes.com, pointed out the challenge of being fast and holding to a high standard of quality:

> To me the toughest thing to doing what I do is balancing the need for speed with the desire to be incredibly accurate, to uphold the long traditions of this news organization and to deliver the kind of quality that people expect from us in print on a minute-to-minute basis.

Online journalists face a tough balancing act with breaking news for multiple reasons including the capacity of the medium, pressures of competition, limitations of resources, complexity of the editing process, and the expectation of the audience that information will be available immediately. These challenges make it difficult to establish an uncompromised standard of excellence in breaking news.

Chapter 3 will explore the balancing act and the challenges and how they have played out through breaking news events including the jet landing in the Hudson River and a rumor that Apple might buy Twitter.

Comprehensiveness in Content: Chapter 4

Online journalism provides the ability to go beyond the text of a story or outside it to give background and present supporting materials. Its capacity for thoroughness and completeness goes beyond what any other single medium can provide. Its multiplicity of forms of presentation allows users to learn in different ways: Breaking news doesn't always revolve around a written story, and different components can help different types of learners. Robert Hood, supervising producer for multimedia at msnbc.com, offered this perspective:

> Here we are at this precious online moment when the story gets to suggest the medium in which it should be told. Visual stories are told with pictures. An interesting narrative can be told with audio and/or video. A process or motion can be explained with information graphics or video. Detail and context can be delivered with text. I think that's fascinating and we need to get better at exploiting the strengths of each medium.

The extraordinary capability of the web for harnessing the best of multiple media means that, ideally at least, journalists can tell stories in a better-tailored and fuller manner than ever before. But plenty of barriers stand in the way. Limitations on staff sizes, thanks to the economics of media competition, mean that few web newsrooms are likely to have the resources to capitalize fully on the depth and breadth of the medium. Time pressures are ever present. And the medium itself poses a challenge: the difficulty in unifying the parts of a story and providing proper context for users entering in different ways.

Chapter 4 will map out the developing standard of comprehensiveness in online journalism and the barriers to reaching it. The discussion, with many examples, will include both the overarching elements of comprehensiveness and strengths of forms that contribute to the whole: interactive graphics, text, audio, photos, and video.

Open-Endedness in Story Development: Chapter 5

Storytelling on the web is remarkably malleable. The story becomes an evolving and organic thing, especially when both journalists and users contribute information that may open up new questions and directions. Stories can evolve in complex ways over time. The capacity of the web to allow for multifaceted growth of stories advances and challenges traditional definitions of story development.

Rex Sorgatz, an Internet media strategist and blogger who was executive producer for msnbc.com before leaving in 2007, reflected at that time on the history of journalistic storytelling on the web back into the late 1990s and looked ahead:

> I think that a "story" has stayed the same throughout that time, for the most part, in the sense that a story represents a snapshot through time of how we perceived an event at that moment. I go back and look at the news stories on 9/11 and I know that those stories were written then, at that moment, and they have these media elements that were available to be assembled. . . . It is a de facto historical record for me. I think that that's going to change in the next 10 years, that the stories become more organic. And if I put on big future goggles, they look a little bit more like encyclopedia entries to me, or Wikipedia entries— look like things that evolved over time.

Sorgatz's comments highlight the evolution in online journalism that has continued since then. The shift he portrayed reflects the open-ended quality of storytelling as it develops in an era when members of the public can themselves act as content producers, contributors, and even editors.

Chapter 5 will examine what the evolving standard of quality in story development looks like in online journalism. The discussion will show how stories can develop in long or short life spans. It will also look at how the melding of contributions from journalists—or those traditionally defined as journalists—and users both enhances story development and creates challenges for editors and producers at news websites. The place of public contributions and news organizations' use of them have evolved through stories such as the London subway bombings in 2005, the Virginia Tech shootings in 2007, and the Iranian election protests in 2009. In this shifting environment, both respect for public contributions and critical judgment are vital.

The Centrality of Conversation: Chapter 6

Closely related to the role of users in story development is the central place that conversation holds in excellent online journalism. The conversation may come through reader comments on blogs and stories, interaction with the blogger, discussion of issues on forums, or comments on social media such as Facebook. The informal and personal voice of many online writers helps make conversation work. The interactive nature of the web makes conversation possible to a greater degree than in old media, and many online users have high expectations for such opportunities as a result.

Straus of washingtonpost.com pointed to the importance of this element of online journalism:

> I think there is an element to online journalism that isn't really as much of an issue with print journalism. That is the notion that everything online is a conversation between authors and readers; producers and viewers have input. It's simply part of the medium that users can and do respond to whatever it is they're trying to say. I think excellent online journalism is aware of that conversation and attempts to recognize it, promote it, and develop it in ways that contribute to the understanding of readers, viewers, users of whatever issue is being discussed.

This aspect of online excellence overlaps with the traditional public forum role of journalism, so it is not foreign to print journalism. But the nature of the medium and the way it has developed—with social networking sites and thousands of active online communities—mean conversation holds a distinctive place in online journalism.

Chapter 6 will examine conversational aspects of blogs including discussion with and among readers as well as informality of voice and direct address to the audience. The chapter will also look at how news organizations seek to maintain high standards in use of online forums. A third key element of the discussion is how news organizations are responding to the explosion of social media.

To look thoroughly at these four facets of online excellence, it is important to consider them not only through the eyes of journalists but also through an ethical perspective that will help in critically evaluating the promise and challenges of their work. The next chapter lays out this perspective.

❖ REFERENCES

About the Online Journalism Awards. (n.d.). Retrieved April 24, 2010, from http://journalists.org/?page=aboutoja

Awards—Edward R. Murrow Awards. (n.d.) Retrieved July 3, 2010, from http://www.rtdna.org/pages/media_items/edward-r.-murrow-awards100.php?g=67?id=100

Bertrand, C. (1998). Journalism reviews. In M. A. Blanchard (Ed.), *History of the mass media in the United States* (pp. 292–293). Chicago: Fitzroy Dearborn.

Bogart, L. (2004). Reflections on content quality in newspapers [Electronic version]. *Newspaper Research Journal, 25*(1), 40–53.

Ferré, J. P. (1998). Codes of ethics. In M. A. Blanchard (Ed.), *History of the mass media in the United States* (pp. 145–146). Chicago: Fitzroy Dearborn.

Gallagher, R. (1998). Journalism professional organizations. In M. A. Blanchard (Ed.), *History of the mass media in the United States* (pp. 291–292). Chicago: Fitzroy Dearborn.

Gladney, G., Shapiro, I., & Castaldo, J. (2007). Online editors rate web news quality criteria [Electronic version]. *Newspaper Research Journal, 28*(1), 55–69.

Knight-Batten Awards for Innovations in Journalism. (n.d.). Retrieved April 24, 2010, from http://www.j-lab.org/awards/about_the_awards/

Kohut, A., Keeter, S., Doherty, C., Dimock, M., Remez, M., Horowitz, J. M., et al. (2009, September 13). Press accuracy rating hits two decade low. *The Pew Research Center for the People & the Press.* Retrieved February 17, 2010, from http://people-press.org/report/543/

The Pulitzer Prizes. (n.d.). Retrieved February 7, 2009, from http://www.pulitzer.org

❖ COMPANION WEBSITE

Visit the companion website at **www.sagepub.com/craigstudy** for links to examples of online journalism.

2

An Ethical Lens for Looking at Excellence

One important facet of excellence in both old and new media is ethics. By one metaphor, theories of ethics offer lenses through which to view people's work in a way that may highlight important questions about its quality.[1] Actually, different theories of ethics provide a variety of lenses such as virtue, duty, and consequences. Although all of these perspectives are relevant to online journalism, this book will focus on one that is particularly appropriate for examining excellence in a field in transition.[2]

This perspective grows out of the work of Notre Dame philosopher Alasdair MacIntyre (2007) but has roots as far back as the ancient Greeks. Two scholars in journalism ethics, Edmund Lambeth (1992) and more recently Sandra Borden (2007), have applied MacIntyre's

---

[1]The author thanks Dr. Edmund Lambeth, professor emeritus at the University of Missouri School of Journalism, for this metaphor.

[2]For general overviews of virtue-, duty-, and consequence-based perspectives in relation to media ethics, see Christians et al. (2009) and Patterson and Wilkins (2008). The theory used in this book is a kind of virtue ethics, but the book will also refer to duty-based ethics in some examples of ethical dilemmas because duties are a common element in codes of ethics in journalism.

thinking to journalism. Excellence is a key consideration in this school of ethical thought. This theory also sheds light on how the work in a field advances or declines over time as its practitioners strengthen the distinctive features of the practice and elevate its standards—or succumb to the pressures that gnaw at the institutions in which this work is carried out. As changes and pressures buffet the world of online journalism, this perspective offers practical insight on the direction of the field. As the coming chapters evaluate the work and perspective of online journalists, this theory will provide a valuable frame for discussion. In particular, the theory will help shed light on how the four standards of excellence in online journalism introduced in Chapter 1 are developing and may enhance the future potential of journalism, as well as the barriers to achievement of excellence online.[3]

Several key concepts (summarized in Table 2.1) are important for understanding MacIntyre's theory of a practice:

- The idea of a practice itself

- The *telos* or goal of the practice

- Internal goods

- Standards of excellence

- Virtues

- External goods and institutions

Table 2.1   Key Terms in MacIntyre's Theory of a Practice

Term	Summary definition	Examples
Practice	a kind of widely recognized cooperative activity through which participants can pursue particular standards of excellence and ultimately reshape and elevate the meaning of excellence	journalism, medicine, football, music

---

[3]Other writers (e.g., Deuze, 2003, and Stovall, 2004) have previously commented on the potential or distinctive qualities of the online medium, such as interactivity, in relation to journalism. This discussion is different because it places these qualities in a theoretical context focused explicitly on both excellence and ethics.

Term	Summary definition	Examples
Telos	a goal, or end, that one might pursue in a practice and, more broadly, in human life	for journalism, "to help citizens know well in the public sphere" (Borden, 2007); for medicine, health
Internal goods	distinctive achievements of a practice that are realized by pursuing standards of excellence	for journalism, knowledge, and fostering community
Standards of excellence	standards of a practice that are rooted in its best traditions and lead to achievement of internal goods	speed and accuracy with depth in breaking news
Virtues	qualities of good character that drive individuals' ethical conduct and strengthen the practice as a whole	perseverance, courage, honesty
External goods	achievements that accompany a practice but are not distinctive to it; have the potential to corrupt practices	profit, status, power
Institutions	organizational structures in which practices are pursued	newspapers, web news organizations, TV stations

Source: Based on MacIntyre (2007), Borden (2007), and Lambeth (1992).

This chapter will spell out these key elements of this ethical theory as a foundation for the discussion of excellence in the rest of the book.

It will also show how the elements of this perspective are relevant to the evolving work of online journalism.

❖ A PRACTICE: THE SOCIAL CONTEXT

MacIntyre's (2007) definition of a practice is complex, but it is worth a careful look:

By a "practice" I am going to mean any coherent and complex form of socially established cooperative human activity through which goods internal to that form of activity are realized in the course of trying to achieve those standards of excellence which are appropriate to, and partially definitive of, that form of activity, with the result that human powers to achieve excellence, and human conceptions of the ends and goods involved, are systematically extended. (p. 187)

For now it is most important to focus on the first part of the definition; the rest will become clearer in the following sections. A practice is a social venture, not the work of an individual. The fact that it is coherent means that others can identify it, although they will not understand it the way its practitioners do. MacIntyre cites examples from sports and games (football and chess) and from work and creative life (such as architecture, farming, chemistry, painting, music). Even family life falls under this idea.

Borden (2007) has shown how journalism is a practice based on the elements of this definition, though the meaning is different from the general sense of ways of doing things (the sense in the subtitle of this book). Journalism meets MacIntyre's definition in that it "is widely recognized as a distinct human activity," and it involves cooperation (p. 26). Online journalism is not a practice of its own but rather part of the broader practice of journalism. As the previous chapter already noted, the pursuit of online journalism comes with particular developing marks of excellence: speed and accuracy with depth in breaking news, comprehensiveness in content, open-endedness in story development, and centrality of conversation. But these elements overlap with the features of old media, although they manifest themselves in distinctive ways in the online world.

❖ *TELOS:* THE BIG-PICTURE GOAL

It is a long road from ancient Greek thought to 21st-century online journalism, but the ancient Greeks provide help to focus on the real priorities that underlie the work of journalism. The notion of the *telos*—an end or goal—figured prominently in Aristotle's thought, which in turn influenced MacIntyre's.[4] Aristotle pointed to happiness, or "flourishing," as the primary good for humans, but Borden noted that this happiness "is more than just human welfare, or benefit, or utility—it is human

---

[4]For excerpts, additional resources, and commentary on Aristotle, see Denise, White, & Peterfreund, 2008.

excellence, 'maxing out' as a human being" (Borden, 2007, p. 16). It is connected with reason and displayed in a person who exercises practical wisdom. In pursuing specific kinds of activity, people aim at different goods—for example, the goal of medicine is health. The idea of the *telos*, then, applies to both the ultimate goal of life and the goals one might pursue in a practice. As Borden (2007) puts it, "Virtue theory suggests that the way to understand ethics is in terms of pursuing a *telos*, that is, the good of a whole human life; the *telos* hinges partly on doing one's role-related work well" (p. 16). What one pursues in a practice depends on one's *telos*, she notes.

Borden points out that when professionals and scholars think about the *telos* of journalism, whether they use this term or not, they often point to journalism's role in democracy. Bill Kovach and Tom Rosenstiel (2007) argued that the purpose of journalism does not change with shifts in technology or technique.

> For all that the face of journalism has changed, indeed, its purpose has remained remarkably constant, if not always well served, since the notion of "a press" first evolved more than three hundred years ago. And for all that the speed, techniques, and character of news delivery have changed, and are likely to continue to change ever more rapidly, there exists a clear theory and philosophy of journalism that flows out of the function of news that has remained constant and enduring.
>
> The primary purpose of journalism is to provide citizens with the information they need to be free and self-governing. (p. 12)

Kovach and Rosenstiel, though not using the terms "practice" or "*telos*," identify enabling democracy as the *telos* of the practice of journalism, whether that journalism is done in print or online or any other form. Jeffrey Scheuer, in a book titled *The Big Picture: Why Democracies Need Journalistic Excellence*, went so far as to argue that "democracy and journalistic excellence rise or fall together" (2008, p. xii). His argument, too, is based upon a central role for journalism—and specifically excellent journalism—in the success of democracy.

Borden (2007), speaking in the specific language of virtue ethics, laid out a theory of journalism stating

> that journalism's immediate goal is to create a special type of knowledge necessary for community members to flourish; journalists produce and disseminate this knowledge in the form of "news." The ultimate goal, or *telos*, is to help citizens know well in the public sphere. (p. 50)

In her philosophy, the ultimate end of journalism is connected to the flourishing of human beings—an important feature of virtue ethics—as well as to other elements including a "commitment to the common good" (Borden, 2007, p. 49). Journalism has a deep purpose, then, that is connected not only to the health of democracy but also to the health of human beings generally. This book will adopt the *telos* that Borden lays out as its assumption about the purpose of journalism.

❖ INTERNAL GOODS: DISTINCTIVE ACHIEVEMENTS OF THE PRACTICE

In MacIntyre's (2007) theory, internal goods are achievements that result from the pursuit of a particular practice. Using the example of chess, he points out that one can achieve goods such as prestige and money by playing chess, but these could also result from many other pursuits. The internal goods of chess—"a certain highly particular kind of analytical skill, strategic imagination and competitive intensity" (p. 188)—come only in playing chess or similar games. These goods are internal because they make sense only in terms and examples from that practice and because only people with experience in the practice can truly recognize them.

Borden (2007) placed journalism with science and teaching in the category of intellectual practices. These have overlapping internal goods: knowledge, inquiry, discovery, originality, and newness. Borden also points out that journalism has a civic dimension because it is concerned not only with gathering information but also with furthering the common good. Journalism is "a *civic* practice, which directs its activities outward to the community, rather than inward toward its practitioners," like chess playing (p. 52). This perspective implies that fostering community could also be considered an internal good of journalism.

These internal goods are not unique to the online branch of journalism. Any journalist doing news pursues knowledge and inquires about situations, problems, opinions, or solutions. Good journalists always act with some level of originality—unless they're plagiarizing. But these internal goods can be achieved in distinctive ways in online journalism. For example:

• Knowledge: Journalists doing multimedia projects can provide more information, including original source materials, and can use multiple forms that best serve the story and help the audience learn.

They can also make the most of online story development by building out a story for its full potential life span. That can give people more enduring knowledge than they might get from short-term coverage.

• Inquiry: Using primary-source materials in coverage can enhance inquiry into a topic by letting users dig for themselves. Interaction and dialogue about stories can engage them more actively in seeking information. Through conversation about stories, journalists and members of the public can cross-check each other about beliefs and factual assertions.

• Originality: Pursuing this good includes "doing your own investigation and thinking" (Borden, 2007, p. 63). Online journalists can draw on a large volume of public contributions of information in the development of stories, but originality means critically evaluating all information and also working independently to search out the truth of the story.

• Discovery: Information from the public helps users to discover new insight and perspective about events, particularly as people continue to add contributions over time and report from angles or locations that journalists may not have been able to see.

• Newness: Online journalists can report on breaking news in enhanced ways when they produce multiple stories in a day in a variety of forms, with care for accuracy and pursuit of depth on important angles.

• Fostering community: Bloggers can build connection with readers around communities of interest by communicating in an engaging way and inviting dialogue. Discussion forums and social media also draw out voices around common interests.

Online journalism, then, has the potential to achieve a number of important goods of the practice of journalism connected with its intellectual and civic mission.

❖ STANDARDS OF EXCELLENCE: SETTING THE BAR FOR THE FIELD

Standards of excellence are at the center of the discussion in this book, and they hold a key place in MacIntyre's (2007) ethical perspective. In his concept of a practice, striving to achieve standards of excellence produces the internal goods of the practice. The meaning of excellence for MacIntyre can be understood only in the historical context of a practice, which over time will progress (or regress) through "a variety of types and modes of excellence" (p. 189). He goes so far as to say that anyone who enters a practice must "accept the authority of those standards" (p. 190). In online journalism, this means that anyone who claims to be a journalist—whether independently or as part of a big organization—needs to think about his or her standards in comparison with the best previous practices of the craft. That argument may be controversial at a time when trust in mainstream news media is low (Kohut et al., 2009) and bloggers and citizen journalists are sometimes producing better work, but it places priority on the value of learning from high-quality work and thoughtful professional perspectives on ethics.

MacIntyre's definition of a practice also means that journalists who pursue excellence will enhance the ability of practitioners to achieve it and even elevate understanding of what it means to do excellent journalism. As Lambeth (1992) described MacIntyre's theory, pursuing standards of excellence in a practice "sets in motion a dynamic by which a practice's very capacity to achieve excellence can be systematically elevated and extended. As a result, new concepts of the goods and ends involved in a practice emerge" (pp. 73–74). Lambeth points to examples from the history of journalism in the latter half of the 20th century, particularly the development of the use of survey research and computer-assisted reporting. Philip Meyer harnessed the power of survey research for analysis in the aftermath of riots in Detroit in 1967. His work produced a clearer and different understanding of who the rioters were. In 1972, reporters Donald Barlett and James Steele from *The Philadelphia Inquirer* used computer analysis to take a new look at cases in the city involving violent crime. Among other things, they found differences in treatment between blacks and whites and learned that the pace of justice was slow. Relating this work to the dynamic in MacIntyre, Lambeth noted that the powerful combination of detailed documentation, use of computers, and survey research raised the standard of excellence in reporting.

This dynamic of excellence will provide an important perspective in the next several chapters for discussing the work of online journalists as they have pursued the four developing standards of online excellence introduced in Chapter 1: speed and accuracy with depth in breaking news, comprehensiveness in content, open-endedness in story development, and centrality of conversation. As a close look at the journalists' work will show, they—like the computer-assisted reporters before them—have harnessed technology in creative ways that enhance the possibilities of their craft and reshape understanding of the goods and the ends of excellent journalism.

❖ VIRTUES: THE QUALITIES OF GOOD CHARACTER

The idea of virtues, too, is rooted in thousands of years of philosophy but has continued relevance in the 21st-century work of professionals.[5] MacIntyre (2007) defined a virtue as "an acquired human quality" whose exercise is necessary for the achievement of internal goods (p. 191). Virtues are not only important to the ethical life of individuals but also vital to the health of practices. They are goods we use to "define our relationships to those other people with whom we share the kind of purposes and standards which inform practices" (p. 191). In particular, MacIntyre points to justice, courage, and honesty as crucial features of a practice.

Borden has pointed out the role that virtues play beyond the conduct of individuals in sustaining the practice of journalism. For example, having initiative and curiosity, in balance with insight into what is real knowledge versus "trivia or gossip," may help journalism to avoid excessive attention to what is new (p. 67)—an important exercise of virtue in the context of the pressures of immediacy in online journalism.

It is difficult to identify virtues in individuals without observing them over a long period of time to confirm whether their words consistently match their actions. But even interviews such as those for this book, combined with an excellent product, provide hints of virtues such as initiative and honesty. The coming chapters will point out these kinds of hints of the exercise of virtue from the comments and work of journalists.

❖ EXTERNAL GOODS AND INSTITUTIONS: DANGER LURKING

These two final terms are closely related in MacIntyre's thought. External goods, unlike internal ones, happen to be attainable through a

---

[5]For additional reading on the key elements of virtue ethics, its relevance to professions, and additional sources on the topic, see Oakley & Cocking (2001).

practice but are not defined specifically through it. They also belong to an individual and become objects of competition in which some will lose out. By contrast, internal goods, though they emerge from a push for excellence, bring good to everyone in a practice. MacIntyre (2007) pointed to "prestige, status and money" (p. 188) as examples of external goods. Lambeth (1992) cited similar external goods and noted that "the pursuit of more and more external goods—salary, celebrity, status, power—can corrupt practices such as journalism" (p. 73).

The corrupting can come through institutions. For MacIntyre (2007), institutions are a double-edged sword. "Chess, physics and medicine are practices; chess clubs, laboratories, universities and hospitals are institutions" (p. 194). The institutions are set up to pursue external goods. Even so, practices need them to survive over time. But MacIntyre warned that "the ideals and the creativity of the practice are always vulnerable to the acquisitiveness of the institution" (p. 194).

Even though MacIntyre himself was not writing about journalism, his words are deeply significant for the state of journalism in the late 20th and early 21st centuries. Almost all American journalists in the late 20th century pursued their craft in profit-making organizations, whether those were publicly held by stockholders or privately held by families. Some of the most thorough and insightful journalism ever produced flowed from newspaper and broadcast companies that made enough money to give reporters time to do in-depth journalism.[6] But the acquisitiveness to which MacIntyre referred began to undo the uneasy equilibrium of quality and profit. Many of the institutions that housed the reporters, editors, and producers pursuing the practice of journalism with persistence and creativity were also producing the external good of profit at margins much higher than those of many other businesses. (For two discussions of newspaper profits, see Martin, 1998, and Meyer, 1995.) But this profit was unsustainable because circulation and advertising were deteriorating, and the pressures on companies—especially publicly held ones—to make short-term profits were increasing.

In the early years of the 21st century, the acquisitiveness of the institutions of journalism, combined with new and continuing economic pressures, hit home with the practice. Many news companies

---

[6]The Pulitzer Prizes have honored many in-depth newspaper reporting projects. For example, the 1999 prize in investigative reporting went to the staff of *The Miami Herald* for a project that showed widespread voter fraud in an election for mayor—an election that was later overturned ("Inside the Pulitzers," 1999). This kind of reporting has not stopped since then, but the pressures to abandon it have increased.

laid off workers or offered buyouts or early retirement—reducing their costs but also taking away some of the most experienced journalists best equipped to improve the practice.[7] The economics of the online side of journalism remained uncertain. Although many of these organizations poured resources into online operations as print advertising continued deteriorating, it was not clear that the online operations would produce enough revenue to sustain the people and resources needed to continue the pursuit of excellence in the practice.[8] It would be simplistic to say that excessive hunger for profit is the overriding factor hindering journalists from excellent work because profit can provide the resources for excellence and because some news organizations are fighting to make enough to survive. Still, this pressure on media companies has added to the pressure many journalists face.

This unsettling state of affairs is the backdrop against which the journalists in this book have been striving to do excellent work. As the following chapters will show, their individual pursuit of excellence is constrained by the limitations of the institutions in which they work.

❖ REFERENCES

Borden, S. L. (2007). *Journalism as practice: MacIntyre, virtue ethics and the press.* Burlington, VT: Ashgate.

Christians, C. G., Fackler, M., McKee, K. B., Kreshel, P. J., & Woods, R. H., Jr. (2009). *Media ethics: Cases and moral reasoning* (8th ed.). Boston: Allyn & Bacon.

Denise, T. C., White, N. P., & Peterfreund, S. P. (2008). *Great traditions in ethics* (12th ed.). Belmont, CA: Thomson Wadsworth.

Deuze, M. (2003). The web and its journalisms: Considering the consequences of different types of newsmedia online. *New Media & Society, 5*(2), 203–230.

Inside the Pulitzers. (1999, May/June). *Columbia Journalism Review, 38,* 26–27. Retrieved February 2, 2009, from Communication & Mass Media Complete database.

Kohut, A., Keeter, S., Doherty, C., Dimock, M., Remez, M., Horowitz, J. M., et al. (2009, September 13). Press accuracy rating hits two decade low. *The Pew Research Center for the People & the Press.* Retrieved February 17, 2010, from http://people-press.org/report/543/

---

[7]An interactive map showing layoffs and buyouts across the United States starting in June 2007 dramatically portrays the breadth and depth of cuts in newspaper jobs (Paper Cuts, n.d.).

[8]The Pew Project for Excellence in Journalism's annual State of the News Media reports (e.g., 2010) detail the economic challenges faced by news organizations and their owners.

Kovach, B., & Rosenstiel, T. (2007). *The elements of journalism: What newspeople should know and the public should expect* (Rev. ed.). New York: Three Rivers Press.

Lambeth, E. B. (1992). *Committed journalism: An ethic for the profession* (2nd ed.). Bloomington: Indiana University Press.

MacIntyre, A. (2007). *After virtue* (3rd ed.). Notre Dame, IN: University of Notre Dame Press.

Martin, H. (1998). Measuring newspaper profits: Developing a standard of comparison. *Journalism & Mass Communication Quarterly, 75*(3), 500–517. Retrieved February 2, 2009, from Communication & Mass Media Complete database.

Meyer, P. (1995, December). Learning to love lower profits. *American Journalism Review 17,* 40–44. Retrieved February 2, 2009, from Communication & Mass Media Complete database.

Oakley, J., & Cocking, D. (2001). *Virtue ethics and professional roles.* Cambridge, England: Cambridge University Press.

Paper cuts. (n.d.). Retrieved May 1, 2010, from http://graphicdesignr.net/papercuts/

Patterson, P., & Wilkins, L. (2008). *Media ethics: Issues and cases* (6th ed.). New York: McGraw-Hill.

Scheuer, J. (2008). *The big picture: Why democracies need journalistic excellence.* New York: Taylor & Francis Group.

The state of the news media 2010: An annual report on American journalism. (2010, March 15). *Pew Project for Excellence in Journalism.* Retrieved May 9, 2010, from http://www.stateofthemedia.org/2010/index.php

Stovall, J. G. (2004). *Web journalism: Practice and promise of a new medium.* Boston: Pearson Education.

❖ COMPANION WEBSITE

Visit the companion website at **www.sagepub.com/craigstudy** for links to examples of online journalism.

3

Speed and Accuracy With Depth in Breaking News

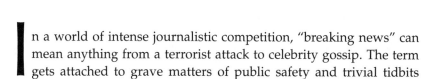

I n a world of intense journalistic competition, "breaking news" can mean anything from a terrorist attack to celebrity gossip. The term gets attached to grave matters of public safety and trivial tidbits about the lives of public figures. Breaking news flows as confirmed information from mainstream journalists and careful bloggers, but it also spews as unconfirmed rumor from those less cautious.

Even though some news organizations and individuals have abused the idea of breaking news, harnessing it uncritically for competitive advantage, at its best it remains a central piece of what journalists provide the public. Sometimes getting accurate information to people quickly may help keep them safe—for example, when wildfires spread or chemicals spill. Or it may help them avoid wasting valuable time—for example, when an accident snarls traffic on an urban interstate. For other events, such as legislative debates or the deaths of public figures, immediate information may not have such a direct effect on people's daily lives. But it may help them voice timely opinions about policy developments or interact intelligently with other people who care about the same events. Because of its impact on people, whether direct or indirect, doing breaking news well is ethically important.

Breaking news always stretches reporters and editors, no matter the medium, because of the time constraints it creates. In online journalism, the pressure to move quickly is particularly intense and therefore the challenges to excellence are great. From the early days of journalism on the web in the 1990s, the capacity of the medium for speed created new possibilities but also new expectations. In the past few years, the proliferation of independent blogs and news sites, along with the development of social media such as Twitter, has provided even greater capacity for quick communication but also intensified what was already a brutal competitive battle in online news. As one blogger put it, discussing reader expectations, "We used to be happy with getting our news weekly, then daily, then hourly. Now we want up-to-the-minute updates. . . . We want instant gratification" (Porter, 2009). Breaking news is one of the key ethical battlegrounds in online journalism because it highlights the tensions between the best traditions of journalism and the competitive realities of the new media world.

This chapter will:

- Describe the battle online journalists face in trying to report and edit both quickly and accurately and to go beyond basic accuracy to provide context and depth.

- Draw on the perspectives of online journalists to talk about standards of excellence in breaking news and the challenges to maintaining those standards. The ethical framework discussed in Chapter 2 will highlight how pursuing excellent work online can strengthen the practice of journalism. This framework will also shed light on the forces at work against excellence and what journalists can do to counter them.

- Provide examples from breaking news that point out the ethical tensions and challenges facing journalists competing in a world filled with social media and blogs.

- Profile the daily challenges one online editor faces on the job as he juggles the responsibilities of breaking news.

❖ THE BATTLE TO BE FAST AND RIGHT: AN OLD CHALLENGE WITH NEW PRESSURES

Doing breaking news well is a longtime challenge for journalists across media. For much of the 20th century, competing newspapers in large cities provided pressure on each other to be first with stories. Radio, with its capacity for immediacy, and later broadcast television brought pressure on a moment-by-moment basis. Wire services that fed all of these media were built on their ability to make rapid, accurate updates throughout the day. With the arrival of 24-hour cable news, news in the late 20th century and into the 21st was shaped by the capacity to be first.

The tension between being fast and being right played out in these media in both moments of triumph and instances of ethical mistakes. Two high-profile examples:

- One of the most famous mistakes in the history of newspapers was the "Dewey Defeats Truman" headline in the *Chicago Daily Tribune* that prematurely declared Thomas Dewey the winner over Harry S. Truman in the 1948 presidential election. Altered workflow because of a press operators' strike, slow election returns, and an unwise prediction by a trusted correspondent converged to lead to publication of an edition with this headline before the election's outcome was settled. In the words of Craig Silverman, who blogs about media errors: "This error is a perfect case study because it includes all of the elements that cause errors on a daily basis: people, process, technology, sources, and the desire to always be first" (Silverman, 2008).

- More recently, reporting on the terrorist attacks in New York City and Washington, D.C., on September 11, 2001, included numerous mistakes and speculative comments. NBC's Matt Lauer speculated live on the *Today* show that some type of air traffic control error caused the plane crashes at the World Trade Center (Ulmer, Sellnow, & Seeger, 2007). CNN reported witnesses seeing a small propeller plane hit the second tower, witnesses who saw a missile, that a fire blazed on the Mall in Washington, and that an explosion was reported on Capitol Hill. ABC speculated that some navigation or other electronic equipment error guided both planes into the towers. CBS speculated that some kind of explosive on the ground would be most likely to bring down the first tower the way it fell; and that eight planes had originally been hijacked, with five still in the air; and that a plane crashed near Camp David. A Washington, D.C., radio station reported that the *USA Today* building was also on fire (Miller, 2002).

Even though mistakes are nothing new in breaking news coverage, online journalism steps up the previous pressures on journalists. Andrea Hamilton, who has a perspective from both old and new media as West Coast news editor for msnbc.com and a former Associated Press writer and editor, observes that a large online news site requires moving at the speed of a wire service but with the additional obligation of exercising news judgment about what goes on the main page of the site. The work is like making selections for a newspaper front page, but the choices come much more quickly.

> The wire service isn't packaging stuff, presenting a whole news site like we are. The AP's sending it out for people to use. So they don't have to exercise their judgment in putting a front page together. They don't have 25 pitches coming at them, like our producers do, from all of our sections—"Hey, we want this sports story out there." There's a lot of pressure on that job. Not everybody's getting all their stories up there every day. You've got science, tech, business, health, entertainment, sports—and news, domestic and international—all competing for those cover spots. And a lot of it never sees the light—or it goes in the sections inside—but it never sees the cover, so there's a lot of news judgment going on. I would liken that more to the newspaper front-page job, only the newspaper editors do it once a day. We do it every two hours.

The ability to update quickly means that producers at msnbc.com have to work every day with a rapid stream of stories that require careful but quick evaluation.

The pace of decision making about stories at msnbc.com reflects the continuing acceleration of the news cycle—the timing of story development, editing, and presentation. But it is not speed of story management alone that marks a shift. For years, journalists reporting breaking news have faced a short cycle for major stories in radio and TV network news and for stories big and not so big on cable news. (See Table 3.1 for a summary of the news cycle for different media.)

But storytelling in small increments has become more and more pervasive. The production cycle of newspapers, with creation of a printed product run on a press, necessitates a lag time of several hours between story writing and delivery of the product. Except for news that comes to light very late, reporting in newspapers appears in the form of a full story, even if some details need to be developed the next day. Similarly, stories appear as full packages—though brief—on TV network newscasts and local affiliates unless they are highly important or dramatic breaking pieces. On cable TV news and for major news on the broadcast networks, reporting often comes in small segments with frequent updates—both in text crawling across the bottom of the screen and early reports read by anchors.

Table 3.1   The News Cycle for Breaking Stories

Medium	Publish/present when?	Publish/present what?	Handling speed and accuracy
Daily newspaper	Next morning for morning papers, same afternoon for afternoon papers	Full story	Confirm information from sources before reporting
Radio news	Hourly; biggest stories immediately	Increments (may include headline, short story, then longer)	Confirm information; may not initially on big stories
Broadcast TV networks and affiliates	Morning and evening shows; biggest stories immediately	Full story; increments for big stories	Confirm information; may not initially on big stories
Cable TV news networks	Often immediately/within minutes	Often increments	Confirm information; may not initially on big stories
Online: larger mainstream media	Often immediately/within minutes	Often increments	Confirm information; may not initially on big stories
Online: smaller mainstream media	Immediately/within minutes on big stories; others may follow newspaper or broadcast cycle	Increments for big stories; more developed story for others	Confirm information; may not initially on big stories
Online: citizen journalists	Varies depending on citizen reporters' availability; may be immediate	Increments using social media; often more developed story otherwise	Varies depending on standards
Online: independent bloggers	Varies depending on availability; may be immediate	Increments	Varies depending on standards
Independent users of social media	Immediately	Increments	Varies depending on standards

Online, incremental storytelling is even more the norm. It is so easy to update a story quickly, and it is so advantageous competitively, that many news sites post short stories initially and then add to or change them throughout the day. News sites using blog formats, whether as their main format or on specific pages, have a natural way to add increments, short or long, as a breaking story develops. With the development of Twitter and Facebook, journalists gained the ability to push out even smaller pieces of stories. And beyond those who are traditional journalists, any member of the public with a cell phone can immediately report his or her observations of a traffic jam or fire via social media—with both text and pictures.

These changes in the news cycle have posed ethical challenges for online journalists when it comes to verification. The handling of unconfirmed information has become a point of tension between the tradition of old media and the fluidity of the new—a point to which this chapter will return. The ability to update in quick, small bites means that news sites can roll out rumors quickly or take the slow route of verification and risk getting beaten on a story.

Carla Baranauckas, an editor on the continuous news desk that has fed NYTimes.com, has handled years of breaking news on the desk, starting on September 11, 2001, the day of the attacks on the World Trade Center. She has seen the pressure from the web's capacity to allow incremental, frequent changes.

> Sometimes we don't put a full 800- or 1,000-word story on the website to begin with. Sometimes we can only be sure of the first 200 words. So we will publish those 200 words, and then we will add to it.

She expressed the inward tension that journalists live with in that environment: "It's always a bit of a tug of war because you always feel the pressure to get something done quickly, but at the same time, you don't want to publish anything that you're not sure of."

The opportunity for updates and audience feedback enables users to look over the shoulders of online journalists. The medium also increases the potential fallout from errors. David Patton, former senior editor at *The Wall Street Journal*'s online operation, WSJ.com, recounted a mistake on the website that spread quickly: In the 2002 election, he said, the *Journal* had developed a new tool to highlight the front page and had placed dummy text in it reporting the election of a new leader in New Zealand. "And, of course, in our haste, we put this thing up without removing all the dummy text and it was out there for about 15 minutes. But, of course, six or seven of our competitors or critics took that moment to say, 'Look, the *Journal* had this up on their website!'"

This kind of viral spread of online journalists' mistakes across the web—even easier than in 2002 because of social media—increases their accountability but also adds to the daily pressure they have to wrestle with in their jobs.

Despite these pressures, conscientious online journalists are striving for a standard of excellence in which speed does not overwhelm quality. The next section will spell out the perspective that emerged from interviews about the ethical standard that helps to drive strong journalistic work with breaking news online.

❖ INSIGHTS FROM ONLINE JOURNALISTS: GIVING VOICE TO A STANDARD

News organizations face great skepticism from the public about their commitment to accuracy. A July 2009 survey by Pew Research Center for the People & the Press found that only 29% of those surveyed thought news organizations "get the facts straight," the lowest in more than two decades of polling (Kohut et al., 2009). Against that backdrop, it might seem questionable even to go to journalists to ask their opinions about excellence in online news. However, the standard that they themselves voice provides insight about practitioners' priorities, even if they do not live up to them perfectly. Journalists at large news organizations express great pride in holding to high standards, even in the face of the pressures of work online. Speed is one consideration for them. But they couple it with other concerns—especially accuracy but also context and completeness or thoroughness. Sometimes speed takes a backseat to these other priorities.

Christine Hauser, a reporter on the *Times'* continuous news desk, was adamant that accuracy trumps speed there.

> Our first priority is always "Nothing goes off unless we've got it right," unless it's rock solid, obviously. That really is our guideline: it's when we are sure of the story. Even if we see it on a couple of wires, if they're reporting such and such number of casualties or whatever, it doesn't matter. Nothing forces our hand before the story is ready— until we on our desk and anyone else in the rest of the building who's providing input is satisfied that what we have is correct.

David Stout, Washington correspondent for the *Times'* continuous news desk, tries to put the value of speed in perspective: "Speed is important, but it's not all-important." It may be a point of pride, but he points out that putting up a story five minutes before *The Washington Post* isn't important in the long run. The key concern, he says, is to avoid being wrong—"especially nowadays, when your mistakes follow you in the cyber world." Taken together, Hauser's and Stout's comments reflect both the desire to pursue a standard of excellence in which accuracy is central and the reality that being inaccurate carries high stakes online.

Bill Grueskin, former managing editor of WSJ.com, points out that in business coverage, an area in which the *Journal* has been known for excellence, mistakes can do damage to readers.

> People don't like getting burned. It's one thing if your paper says the school board vote was 6 to 2 and then you read in the paper the next day it was actually 5 to 3. But it's very different if you get something wrong in the business or the financial section, where people's livelihoods are at stake.

For conscientious journalists, all factual errors matter. But Grueskin's comments highlight the reality that mistakes in business reporting are a matter of particularly high stakes for audience members.

The standard of excellence for breaking news that emerges from the interviews doesn't stop with strict attention to accuracy. It also means pressing beyond factual accuracy to thoroughness and context. Ju-Don Roberts, former managing editor of washingtonpost.com, says excellence in breaking news online means "reacting quickly to a situation and being as thorough as possible." Multiple elements assembled quickly—such as maps, video, and photos—may be part of thoroughness, and fast thinking may help to provide some of those initially from sources such as the AP or a local TV station. "If a reporter is out there," Roberts says, "I think it demonstrates excellence for them to pick up the phone and say, 'Let me give you a quick audio hit of what I see out here.'" But she, too, stresses that "it's better to be right than to be first."

Excellence in breaking news online, then, means serving the audience by providing quick information on location and aggressively working from multiple sources and multiple media to provide a better picture of the situation than only a wire service or text story could offer. It is speed with thoroughness that takes full advantage of the potential of online journalism for breaking news. As discussion in this chapter and later will show, the potential increasingly comes through public contributions and social media alongside the hard work of traditional journalists.

Related to thoroughness is the idea of context. Large newspapers that do in-depth reporting and analysis have for decades placed issues in context with background information and perspective. But as Jennifer Johnson Hicks, a news editor at WSJ.com, points out, online journalism can provide even more context. Online sites have the capacity to follow breaking news reporting quickly with information sources to help readers understand the story better—resources such as links and previous stories on related events or topics. They also can deepen understanding through multimedia elements.

Providing context in breaking news online, however, involves more than harnessing the technical capacity of the web. It means having reporters with the drive and skill to go deeper for answers. Hauser of the *Times* reflected on this aspect of excellence:

> I think that, still, there's the need for really excellent journalists—people who are able, when the dust settles, to think and to know the right people to call to push the story forward—or to present it in a better, clearer way. There still is plenty of room to be competitive—even though, in some sense, the Internet or live TV have leveled the playing field in that sense because we are able to access the same stuff. But that doesn't mean that the story is going to stop there, because what we have to do next is add value to the story.

Giving readers angles that add to the value of the story means employing reporters who understand the need for perspective, know what sources to talk with, and see how to communicate the story clearly. They—and others like them—are necessary for reaching the ideal of rapid communication that also provides meaning and understanding.

❖ BREAKING NEWS THROUGH AN ETHICAL LENS

The development of a standard of excellence in breaking news can be understood better through the theory described in Chapter 2, based on the work of philosopher Alasdair MacIntyre (2007) and applied to journalism by media ethicists Edmund Lambeth (1992) and Sandra Borden (2007). MacIntyre's concept of a practice, which encompasses journalism and other professions, gives a central place to the pursuit of excellence. Excellence in a practice is rooted in its historical context, and the practice moves through "a variety of types and modes of excellence" (MacIntyre, 2007, p. 189).

The combination of technological capability and creative, thoughtful use of this capability—both by conventional journalists and citizens—is pushing journalism into new modes of excellence in breaking news. Journalists have a diverse toolkit that enables them not only to gather and share information quickly but also to do that in multiple forms and combinations. As examples in this chapter and later will show, the modes of excellence are developing through rapid and creative use of these tools. Ethically, the best work has much in common with the previous standards of journalism—rooted in the field's history—while sometimes challenging these standards as well. Again, for MacIntyre (2007), ignoring the previous best practices is not an option, so online practitioners who did not come out of mainstream journalism still need to reflect on those practices.

Efforts to reach a standard of excellence—such as speed with accuracy, thoroughness, and context in online journalism—lead to the attainment of what MacIntyre calls internal goods, achievements that are distinctive to a particular practice. Borden (2007), relating journalism to other intellectual practices such as science and teaching, pointed out internal goods of knowledge, inquiry, discovery, originality, and newness. Journalists achieve these internal goods in areas besides online work, but they may emerge in distinctive ways online. In relation to breaking news, the good of newness is particularly important. When online writers and editors work quickly to produce multiple stories per day in multiple forms while holding strictly to accuracy and seeking depth, they achieve a kind of newness that raises the bar for what immediate reporting can provide for an audience. While they realize this good, they also provide knowledge that is more nuanced than what audiences of newspapers or television might have seen in the same period of time—and this knowledge is based on careful inquiry. The achievement of these goods sets in motion the dynamic that MacIntyre (2007) described in his definition of a practice. Pursuing excellence in breaking news establishes an understanding of a new mode of excellence. This understanding, in turn, enhances the ability of journalists to achieve excellence in breaking news online and recasts the idea of what excellent journalism means.

This portrait of the pursuit of excellence may sound hopelessly idealistic against the backdrop of intense pressure to compete and limited numbers of journalists to do the work, especially at news operations smaller than the *Post, Times, Journal,* and msnbc.com. But even the attempt to work to the standard helps reshape thinking about the best in online journalism. As later discussion in this chapter will show, journalists' individual choices can help counter the pressure of what MacIntyre (2007) called external goods and the institutions in which those journalists work.

❖ ONLINE EXCELLENCE IN DEVELOPMENT: THE HUDSON RIVER JET LANDING

The history of online journalism reflects an evolution toward greater and greater capacity to be thorough and accurate quickly without merely presenting content that would be in print the next day. In the earlier years of online news, it was common for sites connected with newspapers to "repurpose" the content they created with their print product in mind. Some large news organizations—connected with both newspapers and broadcast operations—possessed additional capacity to create and update web-specific content, but the focus across the industry had not shifted online (Lasica, 2002). But as online journalism has evolved, it has realized more and more of the potential for distinctive "types and modes of excellence" (MacIntyre, 2007, p. 189) as news organizations have increasingly taken advantage of the variety of story forms and technologies available. Sometimes, though, the "pros" have watched bloggers or citizens with cell phones tell the heart of a story faster.

The striking evolution in a decade of online journalism—along with the shift in the media landscape toward public empowerment—was evident in *Times* coverage of the water landing by a jetliner in the Hudson River on January 15, 2009. As readers worldwide would find out, pilot Captain Chesley B. "Sully" Sullenberger III saved 155 people by landing US Airways Flight 1549 on the Hudson River after the plane took off from La Guardia Airport and lost engine power because of a bird strike. The story was breaking news that was not only dramatic for members of the public no matter where they were, but also great in its impact on people locally—those who might have loved ones on the plane, workers across the city worried about what happened, and people close enough to the scene to observe or even help with the rescue.

Events and coverage moved quickly:

- The plane took off at 3:26 and landed in the water at 3:31.

- The *Times* posted a breaking news alert on its site by 3:48.

- The *Times* used its City Room blog, which features live reporting about New York City, to communicate segments of the developing story (Belson, 2009). Reader comments on the blog added to the reporting with eyewitness accounts, along with notes of support and reaction. The comments began appearing quickly, with the first time noted as 3:54.

- Details continued to go up on the blog as reporters worked the story. A post at 5:45, with six reporters contributing, led by saying: "A US Airways plane that took off Thursday at 3:26 p.m. from La Guardia Airport plunged into the Hudson River five minutes later, but all 153 people on board were rescued, the Federal Aviation Administration said" (Belson, 2009). Details of what was known at that point followed, including efforts by ferries and other boats to help with the rescue.

- Another post three minutes later (one paragraph) said a news conference with the mayor was coming at 6 p.m.

- Two minutes after that, another post presented a transcribed statement by the chairman of the airline.

- Two more posts during and after the news conference followed.

- As the evening went on, posts of various lengths included information about the pilot, the passengers, and the plane. City Room also compiled eyewitness accounts.

Taken together, the blog accounts enabled readers to get information quickly and with increasing thoroughness without the need to update entire stories.

The *Times* also used slideshows to tell the story from the scene. One slideshow used photos by *Times* photographers and others from wire services ("Plane Crashes," 2009). But in addition, the *Times* invited anyone who had images from the scene to e-mail them. A separate slideshow used reader-submitted photos ("Reader-Submitted Photos," 2009). The reader photos provided additional close-up images of the plane in the water and the rescue. By drawing on the contributions of the public, they added to the power of the visual storytelling.

By using a live blog with its own reporting and reader accounts, and photo slideshows using public and professional photos, the *Times* took advantage of the capacity of online journalism to be thorough quickly. This coverage melded rapid writing in the tradition of wire services with a newer writing form, blogging, and with multimedia elements. It also drew on the expertise of reporters to gather accurate information quickly, as well as the ability of members of the public to add their accounts without being called by reporters. As a result, it reflected a standard of excellence rooted in the best of old practices but embodying a new and distinctive combination of rapid accuracy and detail that did not appear in old media. Coverage like this at many news organizations—on this and other stories—has helped to reshape the notion of what excellent journalism looks like.

But this coverage also points to the challenges traditional news organizations face doing breaking news online. When it came to getting the story out first, the *Times* lost out to a member of the public, Janis Krums, who at 3:36—10 minutes after the plane took off—posted a photo he had taken from his iPhone showing the jet in the water with passengers on the wing of the plane. The photo actually ended up later in the *Times* slideshow of photos from staff and wires ("Plane Crashes," 2009).

Screenshot 3.1   Thanks to Twitter, this photo from an iPhone made it to the public faster than the *Times'* coverage. Later it added to the *Times'* own presentation after it was distributed by The Associated Press.

But the world first saw it through Twitter. Krums sent this tweet:

http://twitpic.com/135xa—There's a plane in the Hudson. I'm on the ferry going to pick up the people. Crazy. 12:36 PM Jan 15th from TwitPic (Krums, 2009).

Thanks to iPhone technology and Twitter, Krums was able to communicate the essence of the story in text and one of the most powerful images anyone captured. What he did, scooping one of the largest news organizations in the world in its backyard, highlights the fact that traditional news organizations will not likely be first in speed in the future and may lose out on the first, best presentations of many events. Chapter 5 will explore in more detail the role of the public in story development. The next section will look more broadly at challenges journalists face in doing excellent breaking news work online.

❖ CHALLENGES TO MAINTAINING AND ENHANCING EXCELLENCE

Online journalists at large and small news organizations all face challenges to their ability to present breaking news with speed, accuracy, and depth. These challenges stem partly from the capacity of the medium itself. They are made worse by the pressures of what MacIntyre (2007) called external goods—such as profit and status—that are an inevitable part of life in the institutions in which they do their work. This section digs deeper into the challenges; the following one looks at how conscientious journalists can pursue excellence in spite of them.

The same capability that enables excellent work online creates greater time pressures. These time pressures, in turn, are wrapped up with expectations of the audience, management, and journalists themselves, as well as limitations on staffing. And the pressure to be fast creates a variety of threats to the quality of the journalism.

Time Pressures and Competition

Journalists feel time pressures shaped by expectations from a variety of directions. Tom Brew, deputy editor for distribution at msnbc.com, is a former newspaper journalist who was present from the early days of the site.

Photo 3.1   Deputy editor Tom Brew, who has been at msnbc.com since the early days of the site, has seen audience expectations for speed in television transferred to the web.

He saw the speed expectations that audiences had for television transferred to the web—with the attendant challenges to accuracy from trying to keep pace with television's speed. "Inevitably you're going to have mistakes," he said, "and all we can do is fix them as best we can as fast as we can." This perspective stands in tension with the traditional expectation of accuracy at wire services, where stories moved quickly but the standard was zero tolerance for errors—even if errors still crept in daily.

Other expectations come, explicitly or implicitly, from management or from journalists themselves because of competitive pressures. Alex Johnson, a projects reporter at msnbc.com, talked about time constraints and linked them to competition.

> The way I describe what we do is we try to do newspaper journalism on radio deadlines. I'm not convinced that anybody has really found the right way to do that yet. I think we're probably as close as anybody in the industry to getting there. But the demand—while we've been talking there went a deadline, there went another deadline.

Johnson sees the challenges of technology as less of an issue than the time pressures related to competition: "Do you cut the corner and not make that extra phone call, or do you rush something up before you've confirmed it just because CNN has had it up for 45 seconds?"

In this perspective, technology may be a temporary barrier to excellence, but far greater is the fact that competing news organizations also equipped to move quickly create an atmosphere in which journalists may be tempted to neglect thoroughness or verification. This kind of competitive pressure, even if it is not stated by management, pushes journalists toward pursuit of an external good of status—in the organization or the industry—of being first. The potential cost to excellence is significant in a practice that, as Borden (2007) noted, gives a central place to verification. Without corroborating of information, journalists cannot claim to achieve reliable knowledge and thereby lose out on the realization of this internal good.

The tension in journalism online between expectations of speed and the value of confirmed accuracy is particularly acute in the realm of blogging—both blogs done by mainstream news organizations and others done by independent people, grounded in the ethical traditions of good journalism or otherwise.

Ashby Jones, editor of the *Journal*'s Law Blog, has seen the pressure of competition play out with that blog. He said he sees time demands as one of the biggest barriers to excellence.

They've done studies on blogs that show that two of the quickest ways to lose readers are to post too much or post too little. So you're constantly trying to put up the right number of items every day. And most of the time you don't run the risk of putting up too much because you're busy, so you run the risk of putting up not enough—and so when you have something, you want to get it up quickly. And sometimes there's breaking news in there—and it's hard, and getting harder and harder with blogs and other online outlets, to be the first to break news. So you're constantly battling competing impulses: On the one hand, you want to be the first to get something up; on the other, you've got to make sure that everything adheres to the rigorous sort of ethical standards that the *Journal* abides by. And so that is something that I feel pretty acutely—and that, I think, is one of the bigger challenges to me.

Jones freely acknowledges that compared with the newspaper, the blog has to run more corrections. "It's something else that I'm not proud of, but it's a function of sometimes trying to get things up quickly and not necessarily having the time to go and fact-check every little thing." So in the atmosphere of acute competition with blogs and others, even one of the news operations with the highest ethical standards sometimes gives ground in the accuracy-versus-speed battle.

Competitive pressures in the blogging world can come from a huge range of sources, both inside and outside mainstream media. These can make the pressure for speed especially intense. Rex Sorgatz, an Internet media strategist and blogger who was executive producer for msnbc.com, talked about the tension between big media and bloggers outside these news organizations, and the pressure on journalists to move more quickly. "Blogosphere loves to point at big media and say, 'Mistake, mistake, mistake!' and big media likes to point at blogosphere and say, 'You're moving too fast, too fast; slow down; you're making mistakes, mistakes, mistakes!'"

Sorgatz said it would be inevitable that big media outlets would speed up their publication cycle. Speaking from the standpoint of big media, he said:

I feel like we're going to do everything we possibly can to follow the old standards of how to do fact-checking and to be rigorous, but there will be mistakes along the way because of the way that the cycle has changed. And I could be outraged, I could scream that that's not the way it should be, I could tell the whole world to slow down. But I would lose.

Sorgatz's perspective provides a sobering warning about the downside of increased speed and the danger that the pressure to be first will erode the quality of journalism. External goods—whether the status of being first or the profit from successful competition—can turn an accelerated news cycle in which excellence is possible into an all-out race in which excellence is the exception.

The tension between old and new cycles and standards was evident in mid-2009 between the *Times* and TechCrunch, a group of websites covering technology and technology business. TechCrunch blogs report breaking technology news aggressively, often beating mainstream media outlets on stories. But founder and co-editor Michael Arrington has a reporting philosophy that both overlaps with and challenges the conventional wisdom of journalism. The differences and similarities came into the open in the aftermath of a June 2009 *Times* piece, displayed online under the headline "Get the Tech Scuttlebutt! (It Might Even Be True)" (Darlin, 2009). The story raised questions about the judgment of TechCrunch and other sites that report rumors before information is confirmed—a practice that the article called a "truth-be-damned approach" reminiscent of the Yellow Journalism era at the turn of the previous century.

Arrington (2009b) struck back on TechCrunch, saying writer Damon Darlin had taken his words out of context. His defense tied the approach of TechCrunch to transparency—a principle, though he does not say so, discussed widely in the study of ethics. (See, for example, Plaisance, 2009, pp. 43–72.)

> We don't believe that readers need to be presented with a sausage all the time. Sometimes it's both entertaining and informative to see that sausage being made, too. The key is to be transparent at all times. If we post something we think is rough, we say so. If we think it's absolutely true, we signal that, too, while protecting our sources. (Arrington, 2009b)

Arrington argued that posting unconfirmed information will sometimes bring sources out to flesh out a story, which he said may not happen without taking that approach. And indeed his blogs do signal their doubts about stories, as was evident in a later post on the CrunchGear gadget blog discussing a report from another site about a launch of a new Intel chipset: The post said the site "makes no reference to any sources, so take the information with a grain of salt" (Aamoth, 2009).

Jeff Jarvis, who blogs about media on Buzzmachine.com and directs the interactive journalism program at City University of New York's

Graduate School of Journalism, reacted to the *Times* story with an eloquent assessment of what he saw as "a clash over journalistic culture and methods—product journalism v. process journalism" (Jarvis, 2009). He argued that putting up posts that are not fully developed says to readers: "Here's what we know, here's what we don't know, what do you know." He sees acknowledging what one doesn't know as crucial. It is "journalism as beta"—releasing an "incomplete and imperfect" product just as Google does. "It is—even from Google—a statement of humanity and humility: We're not perfect." Jarvis criticizes conventional journalism for adhering to a "myth of perfection" rooted in the expectations of mass production—believing that a product that must be produced once for everyone is perfect simply because it must be. In short: "Newspaper people see their articles as finished products of their work. Bloggers see their posts as part of the process of learning" (Jarvis, 2009).

This clash of perspectives and the ensuing critiques illustrate how the ethical perspectives of the blogging world stand in tension with those of mainstream journalism—but are not entirely different. The world of news reporting is not simple enough to say that TechCrunch and blogs like it lack any sense of excellence and mainstream operations like the *Times* have a monopoly on it. Aside from the fact that mainstream sites make mistakes, too, the comments by Arrington and Jarvis reflect a concern for getting to accurate information quickly. In airing unconfirmed information, TechCrunch may draw out more sources to advance the truth of the story more quickly and more thoroughly than might happen with conventional reporting. The internal good of newness might be upheld, and knowledge provided as well. But incorrect information in the interim might cause harm—as Grueskin noted discussing the impact of business reporting. Both mainstream media outlets and blogs may be driven by external goods of status or profit at times in pursuing either one of these approaches.

REPORTING A RUMOR: BUZZ ABOUT A DEAL FOR TWITTER

For people who care about technology and business, it's hard to get juicier than a rumor that Apple might buy Twitter. That rumor caught fire on the web one day in May 2009. And two sites reporting it later caught heat from a writer in *The New York Times*. The treatment of the rumor by one of the sites, TechCrunch, offers a case study in the ethics of reporting unconfirmed information.

The critical *Times* story by Damon Darlin (2009) recounted a post in the wee hours of the morning by the New York gossip site Gawker, citing an anonymous source saying Apple and Twitter were negotiating to try to reach a deal (Thomas, 2009). It noted that TechCrunch, which covers technology news, followed hours later with a similar report (Arrington, 2009a). Both posts drew a lot of traffic and prompted reports on a number of other websites, as well as retweets on Twitter. But neither item was verified before it went out.

TechCrunch founder Michael Arrington opened the post with a paragraph about how hot Twitter was. He followed with a sentence citing a source saying Twitter's CEO had turned away an effort by Google to buy it. He addressed the Apple rumor this way in the third paragraph:

> Today, though, rumors popped up that Apple may be looking to buy Twitter. *"Apple is in late stage negotiations to buy Twitter and is hoping to announce it at WWDC in June,"* said a normally reliable source this evening, adding that the purchase price would be $700 million in cash. The trouble is we've checked with other sources who claim to know nothing about any Apple negotiations. If these discussions are happening, Twitter is keeping them very quiet indeed. We would have passed on reporting this rumor at all, but other press is now picking it up. (Arrington, 2009a)

The *Times* story suggested it didn't matter to Arrington that the rumor wasn't true. The tone of the story was harsh on this common blogger approach of covering rumors, referring to it as a "truth-be-damned approach."

Did Arrington act unethically by deciding to report the rumor before it was confirmed? He vigorously defended his action in a TechCrunch post titled "The Morality and Effectiveness of Process Journalism" (Arrington, 2009b). He criticized the *Times* writer for "suggesting that I reported the rumor as if it were real, and waited until deep into the post to say anything about it being unlikely." He pointed out that the rumor shows up first in the third paragraph—"and the statement about it being unlikely to be true came immediately after the sentence that stated the rumor." After quoting the third paragraph of the post, he wrote:

(Continued)

(Continued)

> There's just no way to interpret this paragraph as a cheap way to get traffic by misleading readers. We say exactly what we were hearing, and what we believe to be true. And by the way, it shouldn't matter, but we've subsequently confirmed that Apple and Twitter were in fact in acquisition discussions, and the original source for our story was correct. (Arrington, 2009b)

To sort out the ethics of Arrington's post, it helps to identify relevant ethical values. In professional ethics codes, those often get discussed in terms of what ethics scholars would call duties (deontological ethics). The Society of Professional Journalists code of ethics cites four values: seeking truth, minimizing harm, acting independently, and being accountable (Society of Professional Journalists, 1996).

- Seeking truth is a value in tension here. On one hand, communicating unconfirmed information may violate truth, but Arrington argues that this kind of reporting can help bring truth to the surface by drawing in other sources. And in the paragraph about the rumor itself, he is careful to say what he knows and does not: There are rumors, one source speaking is normally reliable, other sources report knowing nothing. He also says this report is out there in other outlets already.

- TechCrunch is acting independently by checking with other sources—but not by using reporting in other outlets to partially justify reporting a rumor.

- Minimizing harm is a key issue here. If the information affects people's financial decisions but proves to be false, financial harm could result.

- Arrington is being accountable by explaining the process and approach that the site is taking—but not being accountable by leaving the sources anonymous.

By these measures, this approach isn't completely without ethical merit, but it raises significant questions. So does the *Times'* reporting about the details of Arrington's post because it does not clearly represent how he communicated.

Another way of looking at ethical values is to think about virtues—part of the approach used by MacIntyre (2007) and rooted in the tradition of Aristotle. It is interesting that Jeff Jarvis, a blogger and professor writing in defense of Arrington, points to two virtues: humility and transparency (though he does not call them virtues). Jarvis (2009) argued that it shows more humility to clearly acknowledge what one does not know and to move forward in steps as a process. He and Arrington both talk about the transparency of this form of journalism. However, proper exercise of virtues calls for avoiding excess—and too much transparency may be destructive if it is rushed into with information that later does not hold up. Humility, though, appears to be properly exercised in this approach because it admits the shortcomings of reporting.

Staffing Limitations and a "Fire Hose" of Content

Apart from the direct pressures of competition, news organizations trying to do quick, accurate, and thorough reporting face another source of constraints on excellence: staffing limitations. Jim Roberts, associate managing editor for digital news at NYTimes.com, put it this way in 2007:

> The demands of both the 24-hour newsroom as well as the Internet and all its multiple forms of storytelling have fallen squarely on the shoulders of the same number of reporters, give or take some, that we've had for 20 years. Reporters now are being called upon not only to write stories for the paper, to write stories for the web early in the day. Some are being called upon to submit entries to a blog. Any given day, we're interviewing people for audio. Any given day, we're working with reporters on multimedia audio slideshows. We have a vigorous video unit which is also producing stuff constantly. So one of the toughest demands that we have collectively is feeding all of those different types of storytelling.

Whatever the staffing changes that develop in the future, it is unlikely that the *Times* or any other online news operation will operate with a surplus of employees. And news organizations' use of social media creates additional pressures that Roberts did not mention in 2007. The combination of limited resources and the multifaceted demands of online competition will create a continual balancing act as journalists try to pursue excellent work.

Reporter and editor routines have to change greatly from the rhythm of a newspaper newsroom. With the realities of staffing limits, this shift is particularly challenging. In breaking news, the challenges of traveling the road to providing context can be great even with a single story. The combination of unpredictable directions in story development with pressures to update often creates difficulties for both reporters and editors. (The open-ended nature of story development online—including both journalists and user contributions—is discussed in more detail in Chapter 5.)

There are limits to how fully anyone can process the elements of a developing story. Robert Hood, supervising producer for multimedia at msnbc.com, voiced a concern that the pressure for "incremental updating" produces challenges to thoughtful editing and understanding of meaning. He offered a colorful analogy:

> What is editing? It's like taking the raw contents, this fire hose of content that's out there, that you have to digest in some way in order to know: What is the picture of this story? What is the quote that sums it up? What's the headline that we put on the cover? There are moments when the event is running so fast and updates are coming in via NBC News, via Reuters feed, via AP wire, that it's hard sometimes to really—in the fluid environment that we are, we don't have hours to digest that and go, "You know what the thing about this story is?" and that's what is the lead on your paper tomorrow morning. We're sitting at the tip of that fire hose trying to direct the stream of water, and there are moments where it's hard to digest it and give it meaning. . . . This sort of incremental updating nature that we are in, at moments I think it kind of squishes out that editing function.

Writers, editors, and producers for large and small news sites are dealing to one degree or another with the "fire hose" of content if they strive for regular updates of their news. So the struggle that Hood described at msnbc.com is endemic to online breaking news. The expectations that arise from these institutions, the audience, and journalists themselves all feed the hose.

In the context of the broader traditions of journalism as a practice, the accelerated editing process at some news sites and the lack of a structure that makes multiple reads on a story the norm contrasts sharply with the standard at many print operations. Newspapers—at least those in medium-size and large cities—for decades used setups in which stories typically would pass through the hands of an assigning editor, a copy editor, and a copy desk supervisor ("the slot").

Although that arrangement does not guarantee excellence, it makes it more likely that errors will be caught and writing polished. Web operations, particularly smaller ones, are more likely to work without those multiple layers of editing. Even at the large organizations discussed here, those layers are sometimes lacking. With the external good of profit looming in these institutions, along with the good of being first in competition, it is easier to truncate the editing process than to strengthen it.

Mark Stevenson, senior news editor for msnbc.com, who came out of a background in metropolitan newspaper work, said the structure is in place for two reads on general news there, but that may not happen.

> We have as a goal to have at least two sets of eyes on everything in a story. But it doesn't always work that way, especially when there are several breaking news stories, or even just that we're thinly staffed overnight and all of a sudden you get a car bombing here, an election result there, and what have you, and we only have a limited number of people available. So things do get published with just one set of eyes having been on them, which is not ideal. But part of the reality of having to make a profit in news is that sometimes you're not going to have as many resources as you want to get the job done.

Stevenson's description of how the editing process can get squeezed when news breaks captures the broader challenge to quality that news organizations face thanks to the pressures to produce stories quickly. With the capacity for quick updates and the interest inside and outside the newsroom in making the most of that capacity, it is difficult to justify maintaining a process that stands in the way of speed. His comments also underline the reality that the need for profit puts constraints on the pursuit of quality.

One other significant challenge to the quality of online news, and a help at times, is the more public nature of choices that previously played out inside the newsroom away from public view. Tim Hanrahan, assistant managing editor at WSJ.com, said, "In some ways it's tougher today than it was 20 years ago or 10 years ago because all of your rough drafts or your first drafts are out there to see." Readers now see earlier versions of stories with rough spots in language, versions that previously would have been viewed only in the newsroom whether from a wire service or local reporters. Reporters may hear from readers about questionable wording, mistakes, or improperly credited information. This new visibility and stronger feedback loop may get problems fixed faster than they would have been in a newspaper. In this case, the challenge of handling this feedback and correcting errors appropriately may serve to uphold the standard of speed with accuracy rather than threaten it. Journalism that reflects an openness to listening to problems and fixing them may advance excellence without switching entirely to what Jarvis (2009) called "process journalism."

❖ OVERCOMING THE CHALLENGES: VIRTUES IN ACTION

The voices of journalists in this chapter make clear that there are thoughtful practitioners seeking to uphold the best standards of quality in breaking news from old media while using the capacity of the online medium for presentations that meld speed with accuracy, thoroughness, and context in new ways. These voices also highlight the challenges that journalists trying to do excellent breaking news online face from increased time pressure and the difficulties that accompany it. Journalists also face challenges as well as opportunities because of contributions to breaking news from the public, as well as the questions of thoughtful critics outside mainstream media. Maintaining and enhancing the quality of breaking news online involves looking at conditions on a number of levels. As Borden (2007) has argued, journalism as a practice needs careful re-examination. Individual news organizations and their management have to wrestle with their priorities in an economic climate in which the health of profit-making journalism is uncertain but at the same time threatens to erode the ability of journalists to do excellent work.

At the level of individual journalist, students and practitioners can learn from the example of writers, editors, and producers whose actions in their work roles appear to reflect virtues. As noted in Chapter 2, MacIntyre (2007) saw virtues such as justice, courage, and honesty as crucial to the attainment of internal goods of a practice and advancement in excellence. It is difficult to study virtues by brief observation or a single interview, but the discussions with journalists produced hints of virtues connected with their roles on the job.

Initiative, a virtue mentioned by Borden (2007) in connection with journalism, seemed evident in the comments by some of those interviewed. Stevenson of msnbc.com displayed initiative as well as perseverance in lobbying for a role as an editor after the fact. Though his role shifted since the time he made these comments in 2007, they reflect a strong desire to make things better:

The first half of the day these days my role is basically to be an ex-post-facto copy editor for general news and anything that's featured prominently either on MSN or on our cover. Because we move at a fast pace, and we don't have a traditional copy desk and things, it's very easy to publish something and not notice that it's broken, or not notice that part of it is out of date. Or if you're putting together a story from various sources, or even if you're just trying to keep with wire service updates, errors flow in, inconsistencies flow in, things break. So, I'm sort of sweeping-out-the-flood-with-the-broom kind of role. I've been lobbying for that role for many years, and finally we had enough, there was enough critical mass, there was a critical mass of errors, so that I could say, "See this? We don't need this on our site; it looks bad." . . . As I told you, we had to do something for an editor, and I'm the Band-Aid.

Stevenson could have allowed mistakes or bad links or outdated information to stay on the site and considered it someone else's responsibility or the cost of working at a competitive speed. But he stepped forward and pushed for a long time to get that role established. His initiative and perseverance contributed to the quality of the site's presentation of breaking news. Later, even though his duties changed, he still used the time he had available to point out ways to improve it. (See the on-the-job profile at the end of this chapter for more about how Stevenson faces the daily challenges of his work.)

Ju-Don Roberts, formerly of the *Post*, pointed to virtue without using the term in commenting that reporters show excellence when they take the effort to call and offer to provide audio for breaking news. In doing that, as she noted, they are thinking about how they can make the most of the online medium to get people more information quickly. Likewise, Christine Hauser of the *Times* described initiative to make the effort, once she has done the basic initial version of a breaking news story, to "take a copy of it back onto my screen and really think about it and start to, in other words, somehow become like an instant expert in what's being addressed in that story." Expectations of reporting may be high at these organizations, but taking initiative in these ways still pushes the quality of the news report forward toward its greater potential. These kinds of efforts help to realize the internal goods of journalism online and, as with Stevenson's initiative, help to shape a new mode of excellence fitting for online work. They also help to work against the pressures of external goods such as profit and status to be first and produce most quickly with the least effort.

❖ ON-THE-JOB PROFILE: MARK STEVENSON
FACING THE DAILY CHALLENGES

Mark Stevenson's title, senior news editor at msnbc.com, doesn't come close to communicating the responsibilities he juggles in a single day.

One interesting day, October 15, 2009, illustrates that well and shows the challenges he and his colleagues face daily with speed and accuracy.

Stevenson has to monitor developing news every day because he manages the site's headline feed to MSN—which drives a great deal of traffic to msnbc.com—as well as its feed of top stories for mobile devices. That Thursday morning, he was reviewing a file called "Hot," which provides information that might be of interest across the group of NBC news organizations. He saw a note there that gave him his "first inkling" of the story developing about Falcon Heene, a 6-year-old boy in Fort Collins, Colorado. Falcon's parents prompted what turned into a huge search by authorities after

Photo 3.2   Mark Stevenson, senior news editor at msnbc.com, wrestles daily with the difficulties of balancing speed and accuracy as he juggles many responsibilities.

reporting that they feared he had floated away in a homemade helium balloon ("Feared Lost," 2009).

Stevenson said the note referred to "very preliminary and uncon-firmed info" but said the sheriff's department thought the boy was in the air. Stevenson checked on what KUSA in Denver was reporting, and within six minutes of the note, the station had a story saying deputies were looking for a boy who had "floated away." Stevenson passed that on to the news editor on duty, and a writer-editor was assigned. Seeing that this might develop into a story of high interest, he alerted MSN that "we would have a story soon."

Stevenson continued to manage the mobile headlines, which led with the story—meaning a headline was also posted automatically on Facebook for people following msnbc.com there. And he coordinated with MSN on its display of the story, which became the lead on the MSN homepage. In addition, he continued listening to KUSA as it cov-ered the developing story live. He passed information to the people working on the msnbc.com cover (the main page) and writing and revising the story to keep up with developments.

The story presented some interesting challenges with accuracy. "When you talk about speed versus accuracy," Stevenson said, "the hard part was that what the sources were putting out was inaccurate from the start since the kid wasn't actually in that thing." Later on, the world would learn that he was not in the balloon and was safe—and that his parents concocted the story for publicity (Associated Press, 2009). Stevenson said Russ Shaw, who oversees msnbc.com's general news operation, was skeptical about what he was hearing and told the newsroom to be careful to stay with attribution to sources in headlines and other text rather than reporting as fact that the boy was up in the air. "That was absolutely the right call as it all turned out," Stevenson said, "but it was sort of tough since everybody involved seemed certain. But we managed to stick with that anyway."

A point of tension between speed and accuracy, though brief, came when a sheriff was speaking at a news conference and was being told live that the boy had been found at home. It was not immediately clear who had told him or whether it was certain that was true. "There was definitely a press for speed on that point because it was the huge turning point in the whole thing," Stevenson said, even though the uncertainty was resolved within perhaps 30 seconds. Even that "can feel like a long time." Stevenson recalled that the site went first with a marquee attributed to the sheriff across each page—although confirmation came quickly from journalists and others at the home. Again, care in attribution allowed reporting that was both quick and accurate.

A third area that involved careful thinking about accuracy was finding out more about the family. Searching that others did on the web suggested that Richard and Mayumi Heene had appeared on the ABC reality show *Wife Swap* and that he and a partner had a website, ThePsyiencedetectives.com (now defunct), focused on scientific and psychic phenomena. But Stevenson said it was important to take the time to confirm that these were the same people. That may have meant a bit of sacrifice in speed—though these were easy things to confirm because of video and ABC's own confirmation. But careful verification provided the confidence to report accurate information.

Stevenson's trail of sent e-mail during the balloon incident shows the number of things he has to handle in a day—both managing the news feeds and many other tasks. Here are some of the specifics, in his words:

- Reviewed the proposed new grid for the U.S. front (caught that the '89 quake was Loma Prieta, not Prieto). [The grid is the rectangular space at the top of the page with top stories and other elements.]

- Requested a pic so that I could lead our MSN feed with the balloon story (turned out to be a short-lived lead, since MSN elevated soon).

- Advised video editors and the writer-editor handling the story to update the language on our live video feed from KUSA to reflect that authorities were no longer "scouring the skies" but were tracking the balloon and to eliminate language indicating that the boy had untethered the balloon (we had no way to know that).

- Called writer-editor and news editor's attention to garbled caption on story's lead photo.

- Took the balloon story out of the lead of the MSN feed as MSN elevated to lead for the home page.

- Advised MSN that they, too, should update the "scouring skies" language, which they had in their deck.

- Trolled the web, finding YouTube video of dad and sons, the boys' music video, the Psyience Detectives site and earlier blog posts from someone who claimed to know Heene, etc., and passing those on to the people running the main story and putting together a profile of the dad and family.

- After hearing KUSA report that a deputy thought he'd seen something fall from the balloon, I checked the KUSA site, saw they had a pic showing the "something" and passed that on to the people on the story and the media desk.

- Reviewed several updates of our cover grid.

- Reviewed new grid for World front.

- Suggested to our Creative team a change in the headlines feed used in the footer of the interim versions of our site's redesigned story pages.

- Took part in an e-mail discussion of a proposal on how to handle a feature in redesigned story pages.

- Alerted MSN to boy's turning up.

- Participated in oral newsroom discussion of wording for our display type—was the boy "found"? (no, he turned up). Had he been "in a box in the attic"? (turned out the box report was a misunderstanding). Etc.

- Advised one of our contacts at *The Washington Post* on info that would be useful to include in his story pitches to us.

- Advised MSN producer on offbeat pieces available for possible late-night use.

- Advised a software tester that some test pages she was working with should be made unsearchable so users don't stumble across them (like I just had).

- Notified our operations guys that our "most popular" stories feature was malfunctioning.

❖ REFERENCES

Aamoth, D. (2009, October 16). Rumor: Intel Atom N450 (Pine Trail) to launch on January 3rd? *TechCrunch.com*. Retrieved February 17, 2010, from http://www.crunchgear.com/2009/10/16/rumor-intel-atom-n450-pine-trail-to-launch-on-january-3rd/

Arrington, M. (2009a, May 5). Twitter mania: Google got shut down. Apple rumors heat up. *TechCrunch.com*. Retrieved May 7, 2010, from http://techcrunch.com/2009/05/05/twitter-mania-google-got-shut-down-apple-rumors-heat-up/

Arrington, M. (2009b, June 7). The morality and effectiveness of process journalism. *TechCrunch.com*. Retrieved May 7, 2010, from http://techcrunch.com/2009/06/07/the-morality-and-effectiveness-of-process-journalism/

Associated Press. (2009, December 23). 'Balloon boy' parents sentenced to jail time. *msnbc.com*. Retrieved February 21, 2010, from http://www.msnbc.msn.com/id/34574260/ns/us_news-crime_and_courts/

Belson, K. (2009, January 15). Updates from jet rescue in Hudson River. *NYTimes.com*. Retrieved February 17, 2010, from http://cityroom.blogs.nytimes.com/2009/01/15/plane-crashes-into-hudson-river/?ref=nyregion

Borden, S. L. (2007). *Journalism as practice: MacIntyre, virtue ethics and the press.* Burlington, VT: Ashgate.

Darlin, D. (2009, June 6). Get the tech scuttlebutt! (It might even be true.) *NYTimes.com*. Retrieved February 17, 2010, from http://www.nytimes.com/2009/06/07/business/media/07ping.html?_r=1

Feared lost in balloon, boy found at home. (2009, October 15). *msnbc.com*. Retrieved February 17, 2010, from http://www.msnbc.msn.com/id/33330516/ns/us_news-life/

Jarvis, J. (2009, June 7). Product v. process journalism: The myth of perfection v. beta culture. *BuzzMachine*. Retrieved February 17, 2010, from http://www.buzzmachine.com/2009/06/07/processjournalism/

Kohut, A., Keeter, S., Doherty, C., Dimock, M., Remez, M., Horowitz, J. M., et al. (2009, September 13). Press accuracy rating hits two decade low. *The Pew Research Center for the People & the Press*. Retrieved February 17, 2010, from http://people-press.org/report/543/

Krums, J. (2009, January 15). There's a plane in the Hudson. *Twitter*. Retrieved February 17, 2010, from http://twitpic.com/135xa. Archived

October 19, 2009, by WebCite® at http://www.webcitation.org/5ke8F5 kwp

Lambeth, E. B. (1992). *Committed journalism: An ethic for the profession* (2nd ed.). Bloomington: Indiana University Press.

Lasica, J. D. (2002, April 4). Gut check time for new media: Gleaning lessons from the shakeout, as hard cash replaces high concept. *Online Journalism Review.* Retrieved February 17, 2010, from http://www.ojr.org/ojr/business/1017961940.php

MacIntyre, A. (2007). *After virtue* (3rd ed.). Notre Dame, IN: University of Notre Dame Press.

Miller, M. K. (2002, August 25). Three hours that shook America: A chronology of chaos. *Broadcasting & Cable.* Retrieved February 17, 2010, from http://www.broadcastingcable.com/article/143815-Three_hours_that_shook_America_A_chronology_of_chaos.php

Plaisance, P. L. (2009). *Media ethics: Key principles for responsible practice.* Los Angeles, CA: Sage.

Plane crashes into Hudson River. (2009, January 15). *NYTimes.com.* Retrieved May 3, 2010, from http://www.nytimes.com/slideshow/2009/01/15/us/20090115-PLANECRASH_index.html?scp=2&sq=Hudson+River+plane&st=m

Porter, J. (2009, June 16). Process journalism and its Twitter enabler. *Journalistics.* Retrieved April 28, 2010, from http://blog.journalistics.com/2009/process_journalism_and_its_twitter_enabler/

Reader-submitted photos: Jet in Hudson River. (2009, January 15). *NYTimes.com.* Retrieved February 17, 2010, from http://www.nytimes.com/slideshow/2009/01/15/nyregion/20090115_plane_readers_slideshow_index.html

Silverman, C. (2008, November 3). Happy 60th anniversary, "Dewey Defeats Truman." *Regret the Error.* Retrieved February 17, 2010, from http://www.regrettheerror.com/2008/11/03/happy-60th-anniversary-dewey-defeats-truman/

Society of Professional Journalists. (1996). Code of ethics. *Society of Professional Journalists.* Retrieved February 16, 2010, from http://www.spj.org/ethicscode.asp

Thomas, O. (2009, May 5). Could Apple buy Twitter? *Valleywag.* Retrieved April 28, 2010, from http://gawker.com/5240350/could-apple-buy-twitter

Ulmer, R. R., Sellnow, T. L., & Seeger, M. W. (2007). *Effective crisis communication: Moving from crisis to opportunity.* Thousand Oaks, CA: Sage.

❖ COMPANION WEBSITE

Visit the companion website at **www.sagepub.com/craigstudy** for links to examples of online journalism.

4

Comprehensiveness
in Content

B efore journalism went online, journalists fortunate enough to work at news organizations willing to pay for excellence made the most of the available media forms to communicate with depth and breadth. The best newspapers pursued thorough investigative journalism and ran series with lengthy stories and sidebars. At their best, magazines covering public issues and social trends allotted thousands of words to thoughtfully reported stories. Both commercial TV networks and good local stations invested in in-depth projects, and public television and radio did insightful long-form work.

The pressures of profit and competition in recent years have eroded many news organizations' efforts to cover topics comprehensively. Those pressures have squeezed online operations as well as old-media outlets, many of which operate under the same corporate roof.[1]

---

[1]As noted in Chapter 2, the Pew Project for Excellence in Journalism's annual State of the News Media reports (e.g., 2010) detail the economic challenges faced by news organizations and their owners.

But despite the intense economic squeeze on journalism, creative journalists have found ways to harness the distinctive capacity of the web to tell stories.

Online journalism has the potential to be more thorough than journalism in any other medium. It can provide materials in multiple forms that free journalists from the bounds of text-based stories and space limitations. Its flexibility in form of presentation allows journalists to tailor elements of a story to the ways people learn best. The best online journalism models the idea that the whole of something can be greater than the sum of its parts. The nature of the medium is part of the foundation of excellence online, but the medium's potential depends on the efforts of journalists and the priorities of their organizations. The complex nature of the medium also poses distinctive challenges in storytelling, and these challenges add to the difficulties that journalists face thanks to time and staffing limitations. This combination of factors makes it difficult to realize the potential of online journalism to tell comprehensive stories.

This chapter will:

- Map out what comprehensiveness in content means online. This discussion will again draw on the insights of the journalists interviewed, and examples from them and others, to consider what a standard of excellence looks like. The discussion and examples here are relevant to breaking news but focus on nonbreaking multimedia projects—places where one would expect to see comprehensive work. This look at comprehensiveness will explore the strengths of important forms that go into online journalism—text, graphics, audio, photos, and video—as well as the broader strengths of online presentation.

- Consider the challenges to achieving comprehensiveness in coverage—challenges from pressures on journalists and from the nature of the medium itself.

- Use philosopher Alasdair MacIntyre's theory of a practice to help in sorting out the potential and pitfalls in online work. By pursuing a standard of excellence of comprehensiveness, which shows up online in distinctive ways, journalists help realize internal goods such as knowledge and inquiry and reshape what excellent journalism looks like. But they also encounter roadblocks along the way, partly because of the pressures of external goods such as profit in online operations. Virtues—personal qualities such as initiative and perseverance—are important to overcoming these barriers.

- Profile a multimedia producer on the job to show how she manages the multiple tasks of a video project.

❖ INSIGHTS FROM ONLINE JOURNALISTS: WHAT COMPREHENSIVENESS MEANS

Comprehensiveness in online journalism takes in the distinctive strengths of the forms that contribute to the medium, but it also involves strengths that encompass more than one form. Figure 4.1 provides a roadmap of comprehensiveness shaped by the thoughts of the journalists interviewed for this book. This section will take an in-depth look at this map.

Figure 4.1   Comprehensiveness: Mapping a Standard of Excellence

OVERARCHING ELEMENTS

- unfiltered information: original/source documents and data
- greater volume of information
- enduring background information
- drilling down on one aspect of the story
- interaction/dialogue with audience
- combination of forms—"fullest flowering of media"
- forms appropriate to a story and the ways people learn

STRENGTHS OF FORMS

Interactive/information graphics:

- context
- engagement, immersion, user control
- process
- motion

Text:

- detail (articles, links, captions)
- context (articles, links, captions)
- dialogue (blogs, reader comments, forums, social media)

Photos:

- conveying of visual stories

Audio:

- communication of interesting narrative
- voice of character or writer

(Continued)

Figure 4.1 (Continued)

> **Video:**
> - process
> - motion
> - "narrowly specific"/enhancement of text
> - source talking at length
> - human element
> - interesting narrative
> - documentary style—reporter not intrusive, focus on experiencing the event
> - flexibility in format and length
> - authenticity/not always highly produced
> - high-quality reporting and analysis

Overarching Elements

Comprehensiveness in online journalism means going deep and wide with information. It also means fostering opportunities for interaction and making the most of the multiple forms of communication available online.

Unfiltered information: original/source documents and data

One distinctive feature of comprehensive coverage is unfiltered (or less filtered) information—primary-source documents and data that enable users to take more control. Alex Johnson, a projects reporter at msnbc.com, explains this point:

> When you really boil it down, what I think distinguishes what we can do online is, curiously, we can eliminate the filter and the middleman. Yeah, I can write you a synthesized, well-reported, well-crafted story. But that's not ultimately the same experience as seeing the material for yourself. What I love about this is that I can do both.

Johnson says he uses the tools of online journalism to remove the barrier of "the traditional impartial, objective journalism model in which the person with the byline is sort of a de facto expert, and you have to take that person's word for it." But he isn't throwing out the traditional story.

I write a traditional news story for almost everything I do. But I want to give you as much of the original material as I can, that is appropriate, as is allowable in some cases, maybe under legal things or confidentiality agreements. Essentially I'm showing you my work. It's like I'm taking a test, and I'm showing you my work so you can decide for yourself—if I got to the right answer, and if I got to the right answer in the right way. It's a way of trusting the intelligence of an intelligent reader.

A 2009 article Johnson wrote about the inability of many 911 emergency call centers to identify the location of cell phone callers included a link to a site that provided a nationwide map and county-by-county details about local emergency service capabilities (Mandata, 2008). Johnson said this information let readers see the worst problem areas and "draw their own conclusion about whether we were characterizing the data appropriately." The story shows how harnessing the ability of online journalism to provide data underlying reporting can advance the internal goods of knowledge and inquiry by enabling users to dig for themselves to corroborate and even add to the information an article itself provides.

Jennifer Johnson Hicks, a news editor for WSJ.com, echoes the point that online journalists should not abandon traditional news judgment: "I absolutely think we need to play a role in telling the readers what's important." But she points to the priority of giving readers greater control over how they see information. That might mean something like *The Wall Street Journal's* CEO Compensation Scorecard, a chart that enabled readers to compare compensation of various corporate executives (Lobb & Phillips, 2007). The chart was sortable by name of executive, company, industry, compensation, and perks. This kind of chart, like the external link with Johnson's cell phone story, gives readers the power to inquire more deeply on their own.

Greater volume of information

Giving readers documents to scrutinize for themselves or interesting data to mine is much easier with the capacity of the web for information. Providing these materials on a news site or linking to them increases the volume of information readily available. But excellence in this area still depends on organizations and journalists deciding to invest the time and money to present it. Many stories still go onto the web without realizing the capability to provide vastly more supporting material than is possible in newspapers, commercial TV outlets, and even public TV and radio.

Enduring background information

Alan Boyle, science editor for msnbc.com, notes that online journalism, which excels at providing immediate information, can also provide enduring background. "You actually can have more permanence than you do in the newspaper or a magazine."

News organizations have begun realizing the potential available in current and archived material grouped by topic. *The New York Times,* for example, created Times Topics (n.d.), which offers free access to information on thousands of subjects. The material includes text of articles as well as photos, graphics, audio, and video. For some topics, the feature goes deeper with materials such as introductory essays, documents selected by *Times* researchers, and links to websites and articles elsewhere. An article on the *Times* site itself noted that "those efforts have not yielded heavy reader traffic or much advertising" (Pérez-Peña, 2009). But it also pointed out that Google was experimenting with an enhanced news topic feature called Living Stories (Google Living Stories, n.d.) working with both the *Times* and *The Washington Post.*

These kinds of aggregations of previous stories or multimedia materials can not only enhance users' knowledge in a particular moment but also enhance long-term knowledge because they are accessible over a long period of time. And the variety of material, visuals as well as text, enables inquiry in flexible directions according to users' interests and needs.

Drilling down on one aspect of the story

In addition to providing source materials, background, and greater volume of information, comprehensive online journalism can, as NYTimes.com chief producer for investigations Eric Owles puts it, "drill down" on one aspect of a story. He made the point talking about a multimedia segment produced with a larger project on "Africa's Children: Struggles of Youth" (Lafraniere, Polgreen, & Wines, 2006). He said he had seen an article being filed for the newspaper and focused on one small element of it for the multimedia piece. In this case, audio narration, accompanied by photos, takes viewers

> through the process of—this is a young kid in Africa's day. This is what it's like to wake up early in the morning, go out in a fishing boat, be too weak to do all the work that they're doing because they don't have any food and being exhausted and getting hit and things like that from the people that are supposed to be taking care of them.

The focus of the segment on individual children in slavery brought home the broader point of the package.

A powerful example of drilling down on an aspect of the story comes from StarTribune.com in Minneapolis. The site presented a multimedia project about the collapse of the Interstate 35W bridge into the Mississippi River in August 2007, which killed 13 people and injured 144 others (Louwagie et al., 2007). One of the features of the project was an extended aerial photo of the bridge tagged with numbers showing locations of both the survivors and those who died on and around the bridge. Where information was available, the numbers linked to stories about the individuals, some with video interviews and photo galleries. These stories about individuals enabled users to learn the particular stories of the people affected.

The ability to go deep into a single element of the story is not unique to online journalism. In newspapers and magazines, sidebars focus on stories of individuals who were victims of disaster, explain a complicated aspect of a business trend, or provide reaction in a political controversy. TV pieces are particularly suited for showing the stories of people in difficulty. But the multiplicity of storytelling forms available online means that journalists can use the full range of tools of other media to drill down, singly or together, plus those unique to online work such as interactive graphics.

Interaction/dialogue with audience

Like the ability to take a story deeper in multiple ways, the opportunity for interaction and dialogue with the audience is a distinctive strength of the online version of comprehensive journalism. Ju-Don Roberts, former managing editor for washingtonpost.com, considers this characteristic central in the definition of online storytelling: "What makes online storytelling is if it's dynamic, if it's interactive. That's what I think distinguishes a story from a web story. It's not how long it is." What is crucial is using the potential of the medium, she says.

> Are you giving your users another opportunity to engage with you? Is it a monologue or a dialogue? And online storytelling should always be a dialogue, that your users have some way to give you some kind of input or feedback into what you're doing or other ways to interact.

Interaction and dialogue take on a host of forms. Some, such as photo galleries and video, involve just engagement of attention and clicking, so they are interactive only in the most minimal sense. Others, such as polls and reader comments on articles, involve explicit feedback from users, but they do not necessarily lead into dialogue. Sometimes, though, reader comments on stories get other readers engaged in discussion, and comments to bloggers can get both the commenters and the blogger interacting directly. The development of social media such as Twitter and Facebook has enhanced this aspect of online storytelling by multiplying the channels of communication among journalists and interested citizens. Chapters 5 and 6 will look more extensively at interaction and dialogue with the public, through social media and other means. But this is a crucial feature of comprehensiveness in online journalism, so it is important to mention here. Taken together, the tools for online interaction can help to enhance the knowledge of audience members and sharpen the inquiry that both journalists and users pursue on issues.

Combination of forms—"fullest flowering of media"

The rich combination of forms possible in online journalism—when journalists make the most of the medium—is collectively part of the meaning of comprehensiveness online. Tom Kennedy, who spent 11 years as managing editor for multimedia at washingtonpost.com and 10 years as director of photography for National Geographic Society before that, sees this new medium in development "as really in a lot of ways an amalgamation of previous media, possibly with its own unique twists and variants, ultimately." He borrows from the thinking of Marshall McLuhan, a media scholar whose work was popular in the 1960s (McLuhan & Fiore, 1967). Kennedy says that McLuhan saw television as "a throwback to a tradition of storytelling that was really sort of the archetype from the dawn of time—the idea of fusing imagery with oral storytelling tradition." In Kennedy's view, the online medium continues the fusion of imagery with oral storytelling but also joins it with content based on text. "This is perhaps the fullest flowering of media in recent times simply because being online you have the opportunity to present utilizing all the previously existing forms of media and combining them in new ways."

This "flowering" of journalism online is possible not only because of the individual forms of presentation but also because of the depth and breadth that together they allow. Journalists who harness the aggregate potential of the medium to increase the knowledge of the audience are helping to redefine what excellent journalism means. On a good day, this pursuit of excellence might help to realize the *telos*, or goal, that Sandra Borden cited "to help citizens know well in the public sphere" (2007, p. 50). That goal is in keeping with how Kennedy views the pursuit of online excellence:

> I think the excellence is about exploring the potentialities right now and trying to deliver on the collective promise of journalism as a social force to inform and educate people and to give them tools to lead a better life—however one wants to interpret that.

The idea that comprehensive online journalism might help people "to lead a better life" also points to the broader purpose in virtue ethics of helping humans to flourish.

Forms appropriate to a story and the ways people learn

Paige West, director of the Interactive Studio for msnbc.com, notes that the flexibility of presentation form online enables journalists to present stories in forms most appropriate to the story being told and how people learn. Journalists can choose from any or all online forms to "take a story and tell it in the best possible way as opposed to making it fit into text if you're a newspaper or video if you're a broadcast station or radio if you're radio." The overlap that may come with using multiple forms can work to the user's advantage, West says.

> That gives the user the choice in how they consume their information, and people learn in different ways. So some people are very visual, and some people need to read, and some people need to listen. Other people need to do.

Online journalism is extraordinarily versatile. The best of it achieves depth and breadth by making the most of the forms that provide the building blocks of the medium. When journalists realize this potential, they help users to learn and inquire to a fuller extent than was possible through old media.

One example of this kind of excellence is the *Post*'s "Fixing D.C.'s Schools" (2007), an investigative project analyzing the continuing difficulties in the District's public schools and why the problems persist. The project includes several sets of articles; multimedia segments such as one about eight teachers at a high school with text, images, and audio; question-and-answer transcripts; and responses from readers. One of the most powerful elements of the project is an interactive map database that lets users roll over dots showing schools on a map of the District and compare data including percentage of passing grades, crime incidents, percentage of qualified teachers, amount of delay in repairs, and health inspection violations. Users can also add layers including the poverty levels in the areas of these schools. Comparing even a few dots in different parts of the District underlines the huge disparities in conditions from wealthy to poor areas. The elements in the project are a prime example of making the most of online forms and realizing the potential of their combination. Kennedy puts it this way:

> Whether you're a person who's driven by data or whether you're a person who really needs a narrative story to engage you or pull you in or whether you're a person who is moved by imagery, it's a mechanism of understanding that all those aspects are there. Plus we have the ability to allow for interaction with the reporters who are involved in the series or their editors, as well as sharing stories maybe true about a specific school, so that you've got this ability to engage the community and give them an opportunity to talk back.

This package draws on the strengths of multiple approaches to bring the problems of D.C. schools home to a wide range of users. In MacIntyre's terms, it engages them in inquiry in depth and enhances their knowledge of a problem of continuing and great importance to the District. The creative combination of forms models a new kind of excellence in investigative journalism. It is an example of how online journalism can help citizens "know well," in Borden's terms (2007, p. 50). Newspapers, magazines, radio, and television have often helped to advance this goal through thoughtful and engaging reporting on public problems. Online journalism can easily fall short of equaling the best of these media, but it has the potential to contribute to public knowledge in ways that no single one of them has done.

The next section will look more closely at what several online forms can contribute in storytelling.

Strengths of Forms

Comprehensiveness online depends on how stories are told in the nuances of various online forms including interactive/information graphics, text, audio, photos, and video.

Interactive/information graphics

Online graphics can provide rich context, as the D.C. schools example illustrates. Graphics are valuable not only for that kind of long-term project but also for breaking news. West of msnbc.com talked about the value of interactive maps and timelines for providing context to people who are coming late into a developing news story.

> I think timelines are good; I think step-by-step descriptions of what happened exactly are what people want to know in a breaking news situation. If it's a location-based story then maps are very important, any sort of graphics that give people a reference in context for where the events occurred. If you can combine those two things so that you've got both a map and a timeline together, I think that's even better.

West noted that video and text stories don't work so well for retaining old information along with new material.

> A news report is going to bring out the new stuff all the time on television. A text story—maybe you update a story, but maybe that updated paragraph gets embedded a third of the way through the story that somebody's already read, and are they going to read that story again?

Whether they are used with fast-breaking stories or longer-developing ones, interactive graphics can enhance user knowledge through their ability to clearly present compilations of information.

A timeline on msnbc.com provided context for the economic crisis that hit hard in fall 2008 ("Economy in Turmoil," 2008). West, e-mailing in early 2009, said the timeline was created "to show people the events as far back as August 2007 that had forecast the current crisis." The timeline went up in October 2008 and was updated during the next several weeks as the crisis developed. "The cool thing about this is that it's not just a timeline," West wrote. "It's also a chart that shows the relative levels of the Dow Jones, unemployment rates, home prices, problem mortgages, crude oil and gas prices." Along with another multimedia piece showing users the "Winners and Losers" in the financial crisis (no longer online), this "really helped round out the picture of what was going on for people who were caught by surprise or that may not be immersed in the verbiage of economists and policy makers."

West also says graphics allow for greater engagement, immersion, and user control than linear forms like text and video. Another msnbc.com project illustrating these strengths was the Politics Dashboard (2008), a feature that included maps and information on the 2008 election campaign. A Data Explorer tab—affectionately known as "Dora the Explora," West says—let users pore through a huge amount of information connected with the election. (It now displays a results map.)

We had data on fundraising of all Presidential and Congressional candidates broken down by location (state or county), source (individual, PAC, etc.), and amount. We had demographic data such as population, age, gender, race/ethnicity, income, education, and percent below poverty from the census by state and county. We had the latest polling information by state going back several months so users could see how states were trending the closer we got to the election. We had the voting results for Presidential and Congressional elections going back to 1988. It's an amazing amount of information that you could explore for hours finding interesting patterns and correlations in the data, allowing users to play political wonk and predict the outcome.

This kind of graphic is significant in the broader development of the practice of journalism. Informational graphics became a prominent feature of newspaper and magazine presentations of news starting in the 1980s. Graphics such as the charts that *USA Today* has run for years on its front page strengthen the visual storytelling capability of journalism. Interactive online graphics represent a further step in the evolution of visual storytelling excellence because they not only present information in clear and interesting ways but also empower users to interact in numerous ways of their choosing. The combination of quantity and breadth of data with flexible means of exploration provides users the ability to inquire and learn in a deeper way than they could through other media forms.

Interactive graphics can also be effective explaining a process or motion, as Robert Hood, supervising producer for multimedia at msnbc .com, notes. One topic in which graphics have worked well to analyze motion is sports. NYTimes.com used interactive graphics during the 2008 Summer Olympics to, among other things, explain amazing feats by athletes. One interactive feature (Carter et al., 2008) showed how sprinter Usain Bolt of Jamaica blazed through the 100 meters and set a world record of 9.69 seconds. Clicking through the frames of the graphic, users saw illustrations of his position in relation to other runners along the way, text explaining how he used his size and stride to his advantage, and visual breakdowns illustrating how he moved so quickly. This graphic did more to explain what he did than text alone and also more than a printed graphic showing some of the same motion would have.

Text

Text stories, the mainstay of newspapers and magazines, provide detail and context, as Hood points out. The sites where these journalists work and many others are full of examples of text stories that do this, whether written also to appear in print or only online. Here are two:

- Bill Dedman, an investigative reporter for msnbc.com, wrote a story giving context after a jet hit a flock of birds and landed in the Hudson River in New York in January 2009 (Dedman, 2009)—an event discussed in more detail in Chapter 3. Though not lengthy, the article looked at reasons that collisions with birds are increasing. Statistics about bird strikes in the United States and worldwide provided detail for the story. The statistics could have been presented in a chart, but the reasons with explanation worked particularly well in the format of a story.

- An investigation by *The Seattle Times* documented the threat to hospital patients in Washington State from the antibiotic-resistant germ MRSA, which has been spreading rapidly with the help of inconsistent efforts to prevent infection (Berens & Armstrong, 2009). The project included online elements such as graphics, a slideshow, and a searchable database. But articles with the three parts of this series provided important explanation and background. For example, in the first story, reporters Michael J. Berens and Ken Armstrong (2008) explained the holes in data reporting that allow cases to go undocumented and the deficiencies in hospital practices that allow these bacteria to flourish. A conventional text story like this takes some work to read through, but it provides depth of information that would be difficult to develop without some length of text.

Another use of text that is important in online journalism is links. Hyperlinks are at the heart of the identity of the online medium because they enable navigation to other elements on the site and information elsewhere. Like stories themselves, links can help to provide detail and context—for example, by sending readers to sites that offer expert knowledge, explain points of view, or show how to get help. The Seattle series on MRSA models helpful use of links. It points readers to:

- Consumer advocacy groups—Consumers Union, MRSA Survivors Network, and the Committee to Reduce Infection Deaths.

- Government resources—the Washington State Department of Health and federal Centers for Disease Control and Prevention.

- Professional groups—the Association for Professionals in Infection Control and Epidemiology and the Society for Healthcare Epidemiology of America.

The pages with these links also offer context through brief explanations of the types of information available on these sites.

Links are so much a part of the medium that it is easy to take them for granted, but they are integral to online excellence. A key difference between simply shoveling newspaper stories onto a website and providing added value to users is the decision to offer direct ways to connect with additional opportunities for learning.

One other textual element providing detail and context is captions. Good captions give people concise but vital explanation of what photos are showing and sometimes background information as well. Like articles, captions are not unique to new media. But they have gained new life as a vital informational connector in slideshows that are common on online news sites. They also play a role in communication through graphics, as the previous section noted.

The Washington Post used captions to enhance clarity in a slideshow on its website about the strong earthquake that hit Haiti in January 2010 ("Major Earthquake Hits Haiti," 2010). One photo appeared with this caption:

> With the Supreme Court building burning in the background, a woman walks past a dead body that lays in a street in Port-au-Prince, Haiti, where relief workers have descended to help victims of the massive Jan. 12 earthquake.

The caption provided enough information to explain why the woman was covering her face and what building appeared in the background. It also added context by noting that relief workers had come to the area. Although it is unlikely that readers would not have known about the relief effort at that point, the additional background helped to set up the rest of the slideshow. This information appeared at the opening of the slideshow until later photos pushed it back.

Aside from its role in providing detail and context, text provides an important vehicle for dialogue online. That dialogue may come through blogs and reader comments on them, reader comments on stories, discussion forums, or interactions through social media such as Twitter and Facebook. Text provides a way to engage in discussion easily and quickly or at length. Chapter 6 will look in detail at the role of dialogue in online journalism.

Photos

Photo galleries and slideshows with audio appear often in online presentations. Even though the online medium, like broadcasting, enables the use of video, still images have found a key place in online storytelling through these modes of presentation. Hood, who brings extensive training in photography to his work, notes that still photos retain power online for telling visual stories.

Photos from the disaster in Haiti on washingtonpost.com ("Major Earthquake Hits Haiti," 2010) illustrate the power of still photography online. Scores of gripping images showed pain and difficulties that were everywhere, such as:

- A teenage girl recovering from a leg amputation.

- A rescuer hugging a search dog as other workers looked through the rubble of a cathedral.

- A nun and rescue workers praying over the body of a church leader.

- An aerial shot of makeshift tents.

- Huge crowds standing in line for food.

- A Haitian policeman aiming his rifle into a crowd.

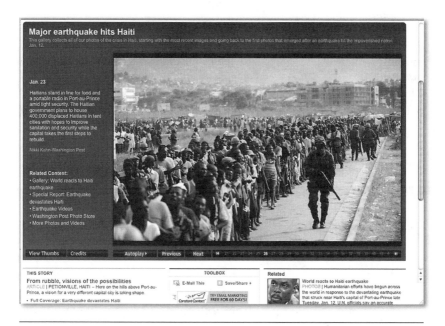

Screenshot 4.1   Slideshows such as this one from washingtonpost.com used powerful images to bring home the extent of suffering after the earthquake that ravaged Haiti in January 2010.

Individually, each of these pictures says something about a slice of the human impact of the earthquake. Unlike video, as frozen images, they enable viewers to focus attention on each one. Together, they work to bring out both the scope and depth of the tragedy as people click through or autoplay the slideshow.

A very different story, but another with visual impact, was the collapse of the Dallas Cowboys' practice facility during a thunderstorm in May 2009. Dallasnews.com, the website of *The Dallas Morning News*, covered the collapse and its aftermath with blog entries, Twitter feeds, video from WFAA-TV, 911 audio, and stories and photos ("Dallas Cowboys Practice Facility Collapses," 2009). These elements work together to give people a range of knowledge in forms that would communicate well to a variety of users, but again the photos play a central role. This was a visually dramatic story, and a gallery helped convey that with images showing the shredded white remnants of the building resting on the green practice fields.

In developing news stories such as these as well as in feature projects, still photos carry a distinctive kind of visual weight individually and collectively.

Audio

Audio brings its own distinctive strengths to online storytelling. For one thing, as Hood notes, it can communicate interesting narrative. For example, a slideshow with photos by Nicole Frugé of the *San Antonio Express-News* uses audio with the voice of Staff Sgt. Daniel Barnes, who had to have both legs amputated after a rocket-propelled grenade hit his vehicle during a road-clearing mission near Baghdad, Iraq, on September 4, 2006 (Frugé, 2009). The story of what happened to him and his feelings about it is quiet but powerful:

- The attack—with a fireball, smoke, soldiers yelling, and Barnes unable to move and blacking out.

- Barnes fighting with medical staff when he woke up, then seeing his wife by surprise when she is brought in to calm him down.

- Adjusting to life since the amputation.

- Wanting to give up at times but thankful to be alive, with the support of his family.

- Making plans for life back home.

The story would have been gripping in other forms, too, but hearing this narrative from Barnes makes it more compelling, especially combined with photos of him and related shots woven in with the sound.

Related to the idea of communicating narrative is the ability of audio to convey the voice of a character in a story or sometimes the writer. Lisa Tozzi, a deputy editor on the *Times* national desk, says:

> The most effective multimedia pieces that we do are the ones where we can give people a taste of the characters that are involved. . . . Our writers are fantastic, but there's something about hearing somebody's voice or seeing somebody's face that can make a real difference in a lot of pieces.

One example comes from a *Times* series called "House Afire," in which reporter David Gonzalez (2007) spent a year with members of a Pentecostal church in a storefront in Harlem. This series includes both text stories and multimedia. An audio slideshow communicates the voices of young people in the church. The audio provides a stronger flavor of these young people and their perspectives of faith. For example, Juan Carlos Matias voices his old attitude toward church: being "forced to go" with his mother threatening to withhold his allowance, not thinking about salvation.

Sometimes audio serves well when the writer's own voice may add insight for the audience. Bill Brink, a senior editor at the *Times*, says: "I think there will be stories where it's clearly preferable to have a subject talking and maybe some where it's clearly preferable to have a writer talking. That may be where the writer's expertise is so overwhelming."

A *Times* science writer, for example, might speak at a high level of expertise about a complicated topic but do it in a conversational way that a general readership will understand.

Video

Video has traveled an interesting road in online news since the early days of Internet journalism in the 1990s. At first, the prevalence of slow Internet connections made it difficult to use video at all in online storytelling, let alone to explore and develop its potential. But in the past decade, video has started coming into its own in online journalism. With the development of video-sharing sites such as YouTube and phones and simple cameras that take and show video, the opportunities to create and distribute video stories have exploded. Engaging video that serves journalistic purposes is produced by veterans of television, transplants from print journalism, and citizens with no training in the field. Compelling stories appear in the polished forms of television videographers and in the raw forms of ordinary citizens.

Video brings a number of strengths to online storytelling, some overlapping with the strengths of other online forms and others more distinctive.

Process or motion: Like graphics, video can show how things work and move, as Hood points out. A feature on auto repairs might show how a mechanic reassembles an engine. Coverage of sports events brings to life the drama of a race down the football field.

Specific enhancement of text: David Patton, former senior editor at WSJ.com, sees value in online video that is "narrowly specific" and enhances story text, complementing rather than duplicating. He points to an amateur video of Asian silver carp showing the fish, which are multiplying in U.S. waters, leaping behind a boat on a tributary of the Missouri River. The video, introduced by a *Journal* reporter who wrote the story, showed readers what these fish do more vividly than the text could have. (For the video and reporter comments, see "Jumping Carp," n.d.)

A source talking at length: Online video can also communicate clearly the thoughts of an intelligent news source. Alex Johnson of msnbc.com says: "I think the best video online, especially in the news format, is verité . . . just turn the camera on and ask somebody an open-ended question and just let them talk." If someone is knowledgeable and has an interesting perspective, he argues, "The best person to give that perspective is the person with the perspective." As an example, he cites a video profile (Brunker, 2009) of Paul Thomas, the unofficial historian of Elkhart, Indiana, where a year-long project (Aleccia et al., n.d.) focused on the impact of the recession on the town. Thomas, 85 years old, speaks articulately about the history of Elkhart and its changes in industry.

The human element/interesting narrative: Andrea Hamilton, West Coast news editor for msnbc.com, points out the strength of online video for focusing on people engaged in activities or telling their stories.

Kari Huus, a reporter for msnbc.com, worked on a story in which video communicated this human element. She wrote an article about roller derby, a roller skating sport in which women with nicknames such as Kim Reaper and Sybil Unrest and team names like Derby Liberation Front compete aggressively on arena tracks in garb such as fishnets and miniskirts. The article is accompanied by multimedia elements including video showing women racing and one commenting in an interview. (For story and multimedia, see Huus, 2006.) Users who click to the video go through a presentation window titled "Wicked Curves." Huus says:

> It's not the best-produced video that ever was, but you can see some of these personalities. And if I just quoted them, you'll see the text and you don't get—it's really hard to convey all the craziness in words.

Video that shows a human element and an engaging story normally relies partly on the power of the audio, but audio alone in a story like this would not easily convey the vivid look and activity of the contestants, either.

Focus on the event, not the reporter: Journalistic video online often uses documentary style in which the reporter is not intrusive and the focus is on letting the audience experience the event. Ju-Don Roberts, formerly of washingtonpost.com, says:

> We feel like our best video is video where the reporter is invisible to what's taking place—that you really are hearing the story or experiencing the event through the participants in that event, or through the main subject of a narrative.

A powerful example of documentary style without an intrusive reporter is a three-part video on washingtonpost.com documenting Inauguration Day 2009. The focus on experiencing the event is reflected in the title: "In the Moment: Witnessing Barack Obama's Historic Inauguration" (2009). This mini-documentary, lasting a total of about eight minutes, has three parts: The first focuses on the swearing in, the second on the inaugural parade, and the third on the celebrations into the night. There is no reporter narration the entire time, and no reporters appear on camera. The focus is on scenes, sounds, faces, and the voices of people present.

Jim Brady, former executive editor of washingtonpost.com, identified the *Post*'s philosophy of online video as "story driven" like print journalism in contrast with the more "personality driven" approach that often appears in broadcast television. Some of the best local television pieces, network TV news magazines, and public television focus on the story in documentary fashion, but commercial TV news does often put the reporter in a more central place.

Excellent online video can still put a reporter on camera when that is important to the story. Ju-Don Roberts points out that the reporter is sometimes needed to explain context in an in-depth story.

Sometimes putting a reporter on camera may simply help to get the audience interested in the story. Newspaper columnists and other well-known reporters may help attract attention and interest because they can build on their connection with viewers.

Flexibility in format and length: Interesting web video shows up in a variety of shapes and sizes. Pieces tend to be brief. Ann Derry, editorial director for video and television at the *Times*, says people typically don't want to watch something the length of a full documentary.

Screenshot 4.2   Many online videos are short, but flexibility in length also makes it possible to do documentary-style pieces such as a 10-minute story about undisclosed accidents in New York State during radiation treatment.

Some *Times* video is longer, though, like a 10-minute story exploring the fact that New York state law does not require accidents in radiation treatment to be made public (Farrell & Harris, 2010). A story like this about medical dangers with life-and-death implications is likely to keep viewers engaged. Length can follow the needs of the story, Derry says:

The thing that we really have an advantage with on the web is that the story can dictate its length. You're not trying to put it into a slot. When you've come from television for as long as I've been, you have to slot things into the time slot. But there's no time slot. There's not even a word count.

Format is also flexible because pieces don't have to fit into the container of a television show. *Times* video work, Derry says, is "informed by all the kinds of things that you do on TV, but you don't have to only have a food network and only do an hour-long cooking show."

Times video comes in multiple forms, including many packages with journalist narration, interviewees on camera, and "B-roll" footage of scenes and activity. Other segments are focused on reporters speaking as experts. The tone is often the subdued style of public television and serious local and network TV pieces. But some segments break out of that and have more fun—such as a repeated feature with technology writer David Pogue called "The Baiting Game." In one, Pogue reviews products in a mock game show format "where we tempt a customer with three delicious-looking smart phones and only later tell her what's wrong with them" (Pogue, 2009). In MacIntyre's (2007) formal terms, these segments in various ways advance the internal good of knowledge, engaging viewers by both serious and humorous means.

Authenticity/not always highly produced: Another distinctive feature of video for online journalism is that it does not have to be as highly produced as a polished television package and, in fact, may appear more authentic if it is not. Adam Najberg, senior editor for video at *The Wall Street Journal*, thinks of online journalistic video this way:

> It's showing people something cool that they otherwise wouldn't see. You can mention user-generated cell phone video in a story, and it completely lacks the impact of seeing two or three examples of that strung together. It's when you do a story on flying carp and how they're disrupting waterways: Seeing that just has so much more impact. It explains why YouTube is so great now. YouTube to me is not journalism: It lacks a really good editor and filter, but what they do is what a lot of media outlets like to do online with the editors and the filters in place. . . . I think a lot of this stuff is still being defined now. The one thing I'm sure of is that it doesn't involve high production value because you don't want to do web video as TV on the web. I think that looking slick is not the point. Being there, making the viewer part of the experience, share in that experience, that's the name of the game and that means it's all about the *Wall Street Journal*

reporter who's showing land mines being detonated by explosive experts in Iraq. It's not a reporter standing in front of the camera with a stick microphone talking about it and maybe showing in ten seconds, that's not what it's about.

What represents excellence in online video may continue developing for a number of years, but it seems clear that strong online video for journalism doesn't require the production polish of a commercial TV package—though that is sometimes present. As journalistic video online continues evolving, it is likely to proceed on a range of paths from raw to highly polished. The prevalence of cell phone cameras and the contributions of citizen video (see Chapter 5) will make plenty of "authentic" video with low production values but important information available. At the same time, web operations that grew out of television news will keep drawing on the supply of more polished video created by journalists trained in television. And news organizations with roots in print journalism may pursue ventures with television as they keep fighting to compete. (See the profile at the end of this chapter for an example of a joint venture between a newspaper-based web operation and a local TV station.)

High-quality reporting and analysis: Even if online video does not look like the network nightly newscasts, it still benefits from the quality of reporting and analysis that conscientious journalists, whatever their medium, provide. Conversations with journalists for this book made clear that they pride themselves on the expertise of the reporters whose work feeds the online operation. Derry sees reporter expertise—whether it be through the reporter talking directly or just doing reporting well—as central to the value added in *Times* video. Her thoughts underline the fact that excellent online video journalism has to be grounded in excellent newsgathering, which Borden (2007) viewed as vital to a practice in which reporting is central.

Comprehensiveness Through an Ethical Lens

As in the discussion of breaking news in Chapter 3, MacIntyre's (2007) theory of a practice provides a framework that helps in understanding comprehensiveness online and how pursuing it redefines excellence in journalism.

A standard of excellence in comprehensiveness online includes provision of source documents and data, enduring background, and generally a greater volume of information. It means going deep on single aspects of a story and pursuing interaction or dialogue with the audience. It also means making the most of the combination of available forms to tell a story most effectively and connect best with a variety of audience members. Major building blocks of comprehensive storytelling online—text, graphics, audio, photos, and video—all have distinctive strengths.

As the previous section hinted, journalists and organizations that pursue comprehensiveness in coverage help to achieve internal goods, distinctive outgrowths of the practice of journalism. In the case of comprehensiveness, two of those discussed by Borden (2007), knowledge and inquiry, are particularly relevant. Knowledge is relevant because journalists who pursue the standard of excellence provide more information and information closer to the original sources. And by using multiple forms in ways most appropriate to the story and the audience, they make the most of the opportunity to add to individual audience members' knowledge. Communication of primary sources also enhances inquiry by letting users dig for themselves. Interaction and dialogue engage them more actively as inquirers.

As with speed and accuracy in breaking news, pursuit of comprehensiveness and achievement of these goods puts in motion a dynamic discussed by MacIntyre (2007) and applied to journalism by Edmund Lambeth (1992) and by Borden (2007). Many of the elements of online comprehensiveness existed in previous forms of journalism, but pursuing them online reframes what excellence in journalism means and enhances the ability of journalists to achieve it. For example, the use of graphics that are interactive and build on databases of public information makes excellence something that more actively engages audience members in exploring the data and drawing their own conclusions. These approaches also empower journalists to report more deeply.

The next section will focus on the challenges journalists face in pursuing this standard of excellence as they wrestle with both external goods and the nature of the medium itself.

❖ CHALLENGES TO COMPREHENSIVENESS

The previous section painted a glorious picture of the potential of online journalism to provide comprehensive coverage. But time and staffing limitations, along with the multifaceted and complex nature of the medium itself, can be enough to derail the best efforts of talented journalists. There is a high danger that the actual product will fall short of the best of what television did with video, radio with audio, and newspapers and magazines with text articles and still photos. There is also a danger that online journalism will often fail to make the most of the possibilities for these elements working together.

Time and Staffing Pressures

The discussion of speed and accuracy in Chapter 3 showed that time pressures and limited staffs challenge journalists doing breaking news. But time to pursue in-depth multimedia work apart from breaking news also is hard to find. West of msnbc.com points out that the pressure of daily news never stops, making it difficult to pursue interactive projects, the area she oversees.

Likewise, Tozzi of the *Times*, who has coordinated producers for the web operation, sees challenges from time and staffing limits—even at one of the largest web news organizations in the United States.

> You do have lots of projects coming at you and not a lot of people to handle those projects. I feel like the biggest challenge we face is just trying to do so many things and do them well.

There is no way to do journalism in any medium without limited time or staffing, especially in the atmosphere of economic pressure in the early 21st century. But these limits still threaten the ability of online journalism to achieve its potential. It is easy for superficiality rather than comprehensiveness to become the norm, especially with the multitasking involved in planning and coordination of multiple forms including some with time-consuming technical aspects. On the newsgathering side, limited staffing—especially in small operations—may mean the same person interviews and shoots video. Writing or follow-up questioning for a text story may get squeezed by the time reviewing and editing, or helping to edit, video.

The extent to which these challenges relate to what MacIntyre (2007) called external goods, such as profit or status, depends on how much the institutions that house these news organizations are committed to investments of excellence for the good of the public. But no news organization has unlimited money, and the broad slowdown in the economy has added to the financial pressures news organizations were already facing. It was evident from the interviews with journalists for this book that they are conscientious and creative in their pursuit of high-quality journalism, even though they sometimes fall short. But the climate of competition, combined with broader economic stresses, makes it difficult to keep excellence at the forefront. For the journalists at small online operations, the challenges can be even greater.

Nature of the Medium

Along with the pressures of time and staffing, online journalists face challenges to comprehensiveness related to the nature of the medium. As the previous discussion pointed out, part of the problem comes from the simple fact that online storytelling encompasses several forms, including some that involve technical hurdles. For example, shooting video means understanding camera settings and video formats. Editing video or audio, or creating graphics, involves learning software that can also be complicated. It takes a complex set of thinking and technical skills to work in several forms at a high level of quality.

But the challenges go deeper. The complexity and multifaceted quality of the online medium as a whole can prove vexing for both journalists and their audiences. Online journalists face difficulty in unifying parts of a story and providing context for users entering and navigating in different ways. Mark Stevenson, senior news editor for msnbc.com, points out that the nonlinear nature of online communication means different users will have different experiences of a story. He contrasts it with the traditional inverted pyramid style of newspaper newswriting, which sent readers on one path from most to least important information. "Then, even if they jumped out they still had the best first or they had the foundation or the assumptions in what was going on." In online stories, readers might travel a different path and see a detail without first seeing the context that explains it. That reality leads to what Stevenson calls a kind of "blind men and the elephant" game.

> You know there are a lot more blind people and there are a whole lot more different contact points with the elephant. But the story is still an elephant, and so we have to figure out ways to convey this is an elephant when we know that people are going to be coming in from the tail, from the ear, from the skin.

The "elephant" of an online story is difficult to build in a way that will aid the understanding of people coming from so many vantage points. Even in old media, users face choices of where to go first. Newspaper readers have to choose among headlines, photos and captions, graphics, information boxes, and sidebars. Television news viewers are locked into a linear story sequence, but in recent years they have also faced more and more headlines and summaries in text crawling across the screen. Online storytelling greatly multiplies the choices, though. That means excellent online storytelling calls for particularly careful thinking about the interconnections among the elements and what knowledge and questions they will create when users navigate them.

That careful thinking must take place not only in the minds of individual journalists but also among the members of the whole team (if there is a team) contributing the parts and overseeing the story's development. Tom Kennedy, formerly of washingtonpost.com, says online storytelling calls for some big changes from the traditional organizational dynamics in print organizations. He sees print newsroom culture as "a culture of the silo where people typically are doing their work in isolation"—with some exceptions such as a reporter working with a photographer—up to a point when editors coordinate things. Online storytelling "requires a much more complex set of coordinations and consultations from the ground up." He likens the level of collaboration needed to what happens in filmmaking. The complexity of coordination and communication online will pose a continuing challenge to organizations' ability to do effective online work that deals comprehensively with stories.

The development of social media as a key component of online journalism has complicated the task of coordination but has also pointed toward new ways to integrate the pieces of an online story. Msnbc.com science editor Alan Boyle, who writes the Cosmic Log blog, talked in 2007 about a phase of online journalism that focused on breaking down the elements of storytelling into their individual components without a full grasp of their collective potential. Online journalists could put together something into a Lego construction, he said, "but I don't think we've gotten to the point where you can build a space shuttle out of Legos." Two years later, he was seeing a different phase developing shaped by social networking. For example, during the memorial service for singer Michael Jackson in July 2009, msnbc.com set up an interface that enabled users to tweet about the event while they watched it on video on the same screen. (See "Live Coverage," n.d., for a look at the interface and some of the Twitter feed.) To Boyle, that represents a shift toward greater blending of elements at a time when online journalists recognize they need to engage people who are both taking in news and contributing to it.

❖ OVERCOMING THE CHALLENGES: VIRTUES IN ACTION

Handling the complexity of choices in online storytelling and the time constraints for online journalists depends on commitments by organizations to strive for excellence. It also ultimately depends on the priorities of the profession of journalism as a whole. But as MacIntyre's (2007) theory of a practice makes clear, individual journalists are key players in the effort to strive for excellence.

The previous chapter looked at ways that the virtues of initiative and perseverance showed up in the work of the journalists interviewed. Those virtues are essential to comprehensive work in both breaking news and long-term projects. The journalists who experiment with new combinations of storytelling forms are showing initiative to try to make the most of the online medium, even if at some level they are spurred on by competition and may be drawing on approaches others have used. For example, Alex Johnson of msnbc.com, who talked about the importance of providing original source materials for users, shows initiative by pushing beyond the bounds of conventional text stories to connect people with information they can evaluate for themselves. By striving for this kind of transparency, he also reflects the virtue of honesty.

Perseverance shows itself in the long-term commitment to excellence on the part of many of the journalists interviewed. Like a number of others at msnbc.com, Andrea Hamilton came from a long background in print journalism including, for her, The Associated Press. Talking about her colleagues who are veteran journalists, she says:

> They're not burned out; they're just dedicated journalists with a lot of experience. A lot of us could be burned out by now with our experience, the years we have behind us. I mean, I've been in this business for 25 years. I could be totally fried and it would not be unusual or unreasonable to be fried, but we're not. We're still passionate.

The same commitment Hamilton and veteran colleagues showed at msnbc.com was evident in conversations with many journalists at the *Post, Journal,* and *Times,* as well as with those at smaller organizations. All of them have been riding a wave of a developing medium with severe financial pressures and the backdrop of public criticism of mainstream media outlets. Some are younger and newer to the business, but both younger and older journalists have pushed for excellence.

Creativity is also a key virtue for making the most of storytelling forms in an era when journalists are still experimenting with the best standards online. Jenni Pinkley, who is profiled below, showed creativity and flexibility in handling a video assignment that might have seemed simple but was actually quite complex.

❖ ON-THE-JOB PROFILE: JENNI PINKLEY
FACING THE DAILY CHALLENGES

For a conscientious online journalist, no story is too trivial to handle with care—including a story about a bar trivia contest. Jenni Pinkley's work on a video feature about the "Trivia Mafia" in Minneapolis shows how many choices and challenges can arise even in what might seem like a routine project.

Photo 4.1   Shooting and editing video is a big part of Jenni Pinkley's job at StarTribune.com in Minneapolis. Even a story that might seem simple can take perseverance and creativity to do well.

Pinkley works for StarTribune.com, the web operation of the *Star Tribune* newspaper. Her official title is multimedia producer, sports and entertainment coordinator, and it is a job with many responsibilities. She oversees production of video stories, including shooting and editing, and helps develop broadcast and multimedia skills of print reporters and photographers. She divides her time among shooting studio shows featuring sports reporters, finding and assigning video stories, and shooting weekly entertainment video in a joint venture with the CW television network. The partnership, in which revenue is shared between StarTribune.com and CW, means the entertainment features go on the website but also show weekly at 10 p.m. on the local CW station.

The bar trivia story ("CWTC Beat: Bar Trivia Is Hot at 331 Club," 2010) is one of those pieces that Pinkley did for the website and CW. Her work on the project over parts of two days in January 2010 posed technical challenges and workflow difficulties. As with the other CW pieces, she worked with *Star Tribune* nightlife reporter Tom Horgen, one of the newsroom personalities the *Star Tribune* has been putting on camera for shows. This week, the story focused on the Trivia Mafia, which hosts trivia nights in bars across the Twin Cities area and was about to celebrate its third anniversary.

The segment of "The CW Twin Cities Beat" is introduced by two hosts, identified as Natalie and Mike. The finished package from the bar, about a minute long, includes:

- B-roll at the bar with sights and sounds of the contest in action, presented in quick cuts.

- Trivia hosts Shawn and Chuck and contestants speaking on camera from interviews.

- Voiceover by Horgen, who also speaks on camera at the end.

To get to that one-minute product, Pinkley shot about 39 minutes of tape over about 2 hours the night of the event, then spent 4 hours the next day in the editing room. Typically for these pieces, she and Horgen write a script ahead of time. On location they move him around to speak his lines and use a hot light to light him. They do short interviews, and she shoots B-roll. On this night, though, their routine met several challenges. Pinkley stated them this way:

Challenge 1: This happened to fall on a cycle when Tom was also doing his reporting for the print story, which isn't usually the case. This would limit his time available for moving around the room to read the script on-camera.

Challenge 2: Further limiting his time, the trivia event was 2 hours long, meaning we had to move quickly to do his lines and allow him time to gather info to print. And I only had limited time to capture the essence of the night.

Challenge 3: The bar was small, crowded and dark with limited access to outlets to plug in the hot light. The bar was also noisy with music playing when the trivia questions weren't being asked over loudspeaker.

So Pinkley and Horgen were dealing with difficulties related to reporting for multiple media platforms and also challenges to quality with both video and audio.

The clash with the needs of print reporting called for some creative adjustment. Pinkley said that for the print story (Horgen, 2010), Horgen needed time to focus on experiencing the event as it was happening and ask questions then or soon afterward without the distraction of tasks for the video story like doing a line on camera. So rather than spending most of the event moving Horgen around the room and lighting shots, they shot only two of his lines on camera, without special lighting, and did the other three lines off-camera with B-roll covering. That way they got through most of the script by about 15 minutes into the event.

Pinkley tackled the video challenges by manipulating several components on her camera (gain settings, shutter speed, iris) throughout the shoot to keep the right amount of light coming into the camera. Those adjustments enabled her to deal with a dark room that was also sprinkled with bright spots because players were writing on white pieces of paper.

For the audio, she used a shotgun, directional microphone to get sound from around the room while she also placed a wireless mic on the main mic stand to capture the hosts interacting with the crowd. As she went around the room, she asked players questions between segments of loud music. The questions she asked would mesh well with the script. Even with the difficult video environment, she had to focus more at times on the audio and just keep the camera rolling so she didn't cut off chatter from the host to the crowd. That left her with more video to edit than usual.

She worked through the editing the next day, but that took twice as long as being at the event. And she had to juggle interruptions because of her other responsibilities.

Pinkley said Horgen and a couple of others who saw the piece liked the way it was paced. She was pleased with the comments she was able to get from participants to help tell the story. The style of shooting and editing for the CW pieces—with jump cuts, quick zooms in and out, and tilted angles—is a sharp contrast with the more subdued, documentary news story style Pinkley was used to. But this is an entertainment piece for a younger audience, so she is working hard to make the most of new conventions.

Beyond the adjustments of style, Pinkley faces broader challenges doing stories that show on television in addition to online. There is less margin for error than on the web alone. "You have to be broadcast ready. You have to be able to troubleshoot problems," she says. The expectation of quality in shooting and editing is also higher.

Pinkley's experience and training have prepared her for her newest work in video storytelling. She has worked at StarTribune.com since it began in the 1990s, starting in a copy-editing position out of journalism school. Along the way she has retrained herself by taking video classes at a technical college, been mentored by an experienced TV photographer, covered years of stories of all kinds using video, trained photographers to gather audio into slideshows, and taken on video training for staffers as well.

Her work on the bar trivia feature shows the level of care it takes to do excellent work. In her view, doing this kind of work well means being able to "balance how much control you have in a situation" and being flexible and creative enough to make needed changes in approach. In editing, she says, it is important to have the courage to abandon something that isn't working. And whatever the story, it is important to recognize that "your job isn't just done when you're done shooting. You have to get into the editing room after you might be tired and really strung out and still make a story out of it."

That kind of commitment to pursue quality, whether the story is a fun entertainment feature or a life-and-death news piece, lines up with what the ethics scholars in this book call virtue. By persevering and being flexible and creative, Pinkley is setting a high standard for online storytelling.

❖ REFERENCES

Aleccia, J., Brecher, J., Brunker, M., Hood, R., Huus, K., Linn, A., et al. (n.d.) The Elkhart project. *msnbc.com*. Retrieved February 14, 2010, from http://www.msnbc.msn.com/id/31369315/ns/us_news-the_elkhart_project/

Berens, M. J., & Armstrong, K. (2008, November 16). How our hospitals unleashed a MRSA epidemic. *The Seattle Times*. Retrieved February 14, 2010, from http://seattletimes.nwsource.com/html/localnews/2008396215_mrsa day1.html

Berens, M. J., & Armstrong, K. (2009, May 8). Culture of resistance. *The Seattle Times*. Retrieved February 14, 2010, from http://seattletimes.nwsource.com/html/mrsa/

Borden, S. L. (2007). *Journalism as practice: MacIntyre, virtue ethics and the press*. Burlington, VT: Ashgate.

Brunker, M. (2009, July 15). Paul Thomas: Unofficial historian is town's loudest cheerleader. *msnbc.com*. Retrieved February 14, 2010, from http://www.msnbc.msn.com/id/31912307/#29982267

Carter, S., Peçana, S., Roberts, G., Saget, B., Schmidt, M., & Ward, J. (2008, August 19). Bolt's record in the 100 meters. *NYTimes.com*. Retrieved

February 14, 2010, from http://www.nytimes.com/interactive/2008/08/ 16/sports/olympics/20080816_mens100_graphic.html?scp=1&sq= Interactive graphics Olympics bolt&st=cse

CWTC beat: Bar trivia is hot at 331 Club. (2010, January 15). *StarTribune.com*. Retrieved February 14, 2010, from http://www.startribune.com/video/? vid=81511477&show=40448432&elr=KArks5PhDcUUU5PhDco8P77jyPhU

Dallas Cowboys practice facility collapses. (2009). *Dallasnews.com*. Retrieved February 14, 2010, from http://www.dallasnews.com/sharedcontent/dws/ spt/football/cowboys/entry/collapse.html

Dedman, B. (2009, January 16). Bird strikes becoming a more serious threat. *msnbc.com*. Retrieved February 14, 2009, from http://www.msnbc.msn .com/id/28679145/

Economy in turmoil: How the global financial crisis has unfolded. (2008, November 24). *msnbc.com*. Retrieved February 14, 2010, from http://www .msnbc.msn.com/id/26797480

Farrell, S. P., & Harris, R. (2010, January 24). Hidden danger. *NYTimes.com*. Retrieved February 14, 2010, from http://video.nytimes.com/video/ 2009/02/27/us/1247466680985/hidden-danger.html?scp=1&sq= radiation&st=cse

Fixing D.C.'s schools. (2007). *washingtonpost.com*. Retrieved February 14, 2010, from http://www.washingtonpost.com/wp-srv/metro/interactives/dcschools/

Frugé, N. (2009). Carrying on. *Conflictphotos.com*. Retrieved February 14, 2010, from http://conflictphotos.com/blog/wp-content/gallery/Multimedia/ carrying on/

Gonzales, D. (2007, January 16). House afire: A three-part series. *NYTimes.com*. Retrieved February 14, 2010, from http://www.nytimes.com/ref/nyregion/ houseafire_index.html

Google Living Stories. (n.d.). Retrieved February 14, 2010, from http://living stories.googlelabs.com/

Horgen, T. (2010, January 15). Nightlife: Thinking and drinking. *StarTribune .com*. Retrieved February 14, 2010, from http://www.startribune.com/ entertainment/dining/81334787.html?elr=KArksUUUU

Huus, K. (2006, June 23). Fast girls on wheels give roller derby a new spin. *msnbc.com*. Retrieved February 14, 2010, from http://www.msnbc.msn .com/id/13154600

In the moment: Witnessing Barack Obama's historic inauguration. (2009). *washingtonpost.com*. Retrieved February 14, 2010, from http://www .washingtonpost.com/wp-srv/metro/interactives/inauguration09/ video/index.html

Johnson, A. (2009, July 13). Some 911 centers can't keep tabs on cell phones. *msnbc.com*. Retrieved January 25, 2010, from http://www.msnbc.msn .com/id/31786185/

Jumping carp. (n.d.). *WSJ.com*. Retrieved February 22, 2010, from http://online .wsj.com/public/page/8_0006.html?bcpid=86195573&bclid=86272812& bctid=302033962

Lafraniere, S., Polgreen, L., & Wines, M. (2006, March 8). Africa's children: Struggles of youth. *NYTimes.com.* Retrieved February 14, 2010, from http://www.nytimes.com/packages/html/world/20060308_AFRICA CHILD_FEATURE/blocker.html

Lambeth, E. B. (1992). *Committed journalism: An ethic for the profession* (2nd ed.). Bloomington: Indiana University Press.

Live coverage. (n.d.). *msnbc.com.* Retrieved February 14, 2010, from http://www.msnbc.msn.com/id/31768552

Lobb, A., & Phillips, M. (2007). CEO compensation scorecard. *WSJ.com.* Retrieved February 14, 2010, from http://online.wsj.com/public/resources/documents/info-payPerks07-sort.html

Louwagie, P., Friedmann, J., Shiffer, J., Prast, R., Hutt, J., Braunger, D., et al. (2007, December 5). 13 seconds in August: The 35W bridge collapse. *StarTribune.com.* Retrieved February 14, 2010, from http://www.startribune.com/local/12166286.html?var=nocache

MacIntyre, A. (2007). *After virtue* (3rd ed.). Notre Dame, IN: University of Notre Dame Press.

Major earthquake hits Haiti. (2010). *washingtonpost.com.* Retrieved January 25, 2010, from http://www.washingtonpost.com/wp-dyn/content/gallery/2010/01/12/GA2010011203712.html

Mandata, H. (2008). *National Emergency Number Association and DDTI present: 9–1–1 deployment reports & maps.* Columbus, OH: Digital Data Technologies. Retrieved January 25, 2010, from http://nena.ddti.net/

McLuhan, M., & Fiore, Q. (1967). *The medium is the massage.* New York: Bantam.

Pérez-Peña, R. (2009, December 8). Google unveils news-by-topic service. *NYTimes.com.* Retrieved February 14, 2010, from http://www.nytimes.com/2009/12/09/technology/companies/09google.html?_r=1

Pogue, D. (2009, October 29). The baiting game. *NYTimes.com.* Retrieved February 14, 2010, from http://video.nytimes.com/video/2009/10/29/technology/personaltech/1247465422744/the-baiting-game.html?scp=1&sq=pogue%20baiting%20game&st=cse

Politics dashboard. (2008). *msnbc.com.* Retrieved February 14, 2010, from http://www.msnbc.msn.com/id/27105655

The state of the news media 2010: An annual report on American journalism. (2010, March 15). *Pew Project for Excellence in Journalism.* Retrieved May 9, 2010, from http://www.stateofthemedia.org/2010/index.php

Times topics. (n.d.). *NYTimes.com.* Retrieved February 14, 2010, from http://topics.nytimes.com/topics/reference/timestopics/index.html

❖ COMPANION WEBSITE

Visit the companion website at **www.sagepub.com/craigstudy** for links to examples of online journalism.

5

Open-Endedness in
Story Development

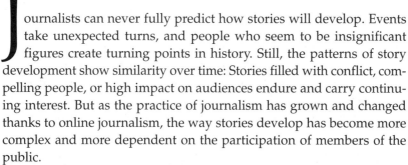

J ournalists can never fully predict how stories will develop. Events take unexpected turns, and people who seem to be insignificant figures create turning points in history. Still, the patterns of story development show similarity over time: Stories filled with conflict, compelling people, or high impact on audiences endure and carry continuing interest. But as the practice of journalism has grown and changed thanks to online journalism, the way stories develop has become more complex and more dependent on the participation of members of the public.

This chapter will:

- Examine features of excellence through which journalists are making the most of the open-ended possibilities in online story development. Examples from online news organizations will show what strong work looks like as it develops over the life span of the story, often with contributions from the public.

- Consider the importance of both critical judgment by journalists about user-generated content (UGC) and openness to what the public can bring to light with cell phone cameras and social media like Twitter.

- Look at personal qualities of journalists needed to do excellent work in this fast-changing environment.

- Profile a social media editor on the job to show how he dealt with a major developing story.

- Again use MacIntyre's (2007) theory of a practice to help shed light on the dynamic of excellence and the challenges to excellence.

The issues in this chapter overlap with the ones in the previous two chapters, but the focus here is on what happens to stories over their full life span, not just as they are breaking or at a snapshot in time, and on how contributions of users become an integral part of the story.

❖ EXCELLENCE IN STORY DEVELOPMENT ONLINE

The continuing story is a well-developed tradition in old media. The story might be the aftermath of a jet crash with rescue, grieving, and investigation or a landmark election with anniversaries as natural points to keep reflecting back on its meaning. Or it might be a victory or tragedy in sports. But in online journalism, stories can develop in a more open-ended manner than they did in old media. It is much easier to add and modify pieces over the life of the story. The pieces can come in all of the forms of old media (text stories, photos, video, audio) plus some new or modified ones (interactive graphics, blogs, tweets). Journalists can mix and match those forms in a huge number of combinations. It is also much easier to draw in the public's accounts, opinions, and images in large numbers—and public contributions have become a normal part of online stories. Public contributions may provide a lot of new information that sends the story in new directions as reporters or other people dig deeper. Or the public may offer opinions and reaction rather than facts, or may react little and bring the story to a close. Journalists may keep gathering news aggressively themselves, or they may write only the first chapter and leave the public with unanswered questions. In both form and content, how a story will evolve and for how long are less predictable than they were in old media.

The difference between old and new media in this area is partly a matter of degree rather than substance because new communication technologies—such as texting, cell phone video, and Twitter—are sources of content that can also feed old media. For example, still images from citizen video can be used in print or on television. But the combination of the qualities of the medium and the online culture's openness to public contributions makes for a substantive difference in how central the role of content from the public is.

Although the online medium is conducive to this open-ended development, this aspect of journalistic practice means not just recognizing the possibilities but also harnessing them to their full potential with careful scrutiny. The interviews with journalists point to three features of excellent work related to this aspect of online journalism:

- Pursuing story development in multiple stages that are in line with the life span of a story.

- Treating public contributions as integral, not peripheral, to the storytelling.

- Keeping a critical eye on user contributions while at the same time respecting the public's sophistication and ability.

This section will look at these three features, with thoughts from journalists and examples.

Multiple Stages in Line With Life Span

Some events merit attention for only a short time; others justify longer-term work. Paul Compton, creative director for washingtonpost.com, calls the difference a matter of "life span" and says online journalists need to develop stories in stages accordingly.

> On the web we think in terms of things in stages, and when you do that you have to think about: What's the life span of this story? Is this something that's going to come and go and then people are going to forget about tomorrow? Or . . . this is going to be most likely a major event that's going to be followed for weeks or months?

If the story is likely to draw long-term interest, he says, "You start to think of things at more incremental levels and how you're going to build it deeper and deeper." So depending on the life span of the story, online journalists may produce a quick, simple presentation in a stage or two, or keep building out to more. Part of excellent work online is discerning the number of stages appropriate to each story. It also means timing the stages in a way that serves the audience in both the short term and the long term—neither putting off the initial reporting too long nor dropping the longer-term development.

The judgments needed are different from what they are in the world of print journalism. As Compton notes, print journalism often means presenting things in one shot. There might be several elements in the presentation—such as a text story, photos, and graphics—but what might make up multiple stages online may appear together in print. Big stories in newspapers may also roll out in stages—with a "first day" treatment focusing on the event and subsequent days' reports focusing on reaction or investigation (as with a plane crash, for example). But online journalism is more conducive to numerous stages timed more closely to the story and the needs of the audience.

For *The Washington Post*, the inauguration of Barack Obama was a major story appropriately covered in several stages online because of its historical importance and its location in Washington, D.C. (see Inauguration Central, 2009).

Compton says it was important to get a gateway page for inauguration material up early to help drive search traffic to the site. The focus of content in the early stage was logistical details such as road closings and what events would occur when.

Pre-designing elements of web presentation helped to smooth out preparation for Inauguration Day itself. That day alone was broken into several stages including the swearing in, the parade, and the evening activities. For Inauguration Day coverage, the organization drew on the resources not only of its staff but also of members of the public. The *Post* enabled people to submit content such as photos from the Mall, where the inauguration took place—trying to make the most of the vantage points of people who were there.

The next day was a kind of stage of its own, with the launch of what Compton calls some of the best material that took time to assemble, such as video that was carefully edited.

The site continued running related news stories in the days after the event. But once the media coverage of the day was past, Compton says, the focus turned to archiving material so users could find it easily in the future. He draws a parallel to the site's treatment of the Watergate scandal of the Nixon administration, in which the *Post*'s newspaper coverage had been crucial, and the more recent development when the identity of the anonymous source Deep Throat was made public.

> Some content that we have kind of lives on our site. Like we have a Watergate section, and that's something that will live forever on the *Post* site, because there are always going to be people who want to see what we have on Watergate, but not much is happening with it anymore. When Deep Throat was revealed, that kind of came back up

in the news again. The inauguration will be continuously on our site and will be available, but we probably won't put too much effort into it anymore.

The inauguration coverage, then, played out in the days leading up to Inauguration Day itself, intensified on the day of it and the following, and lived on long-term as a historic event for which the *Post* had a close-up view. The multiple stages were appropriate to the story and its significance to the site's local and national audiences. The timing of the stages served both the short-term and long-term interests of the audience because early reporting of practical details helped people leading up to the event and long-term life for the coverage satisfied later, more historical interest.

Stories that deserve shorter life spans are more numerous than ones with great long-term historical value, though many stories in particular communities retain that kind of importance for those local areas. Pieces on a huge range of topics, from thunderstorm damage reports to restaurant reviews, may go out of date quickly but not be major enough to deserve updating or a new story.

Public Contributions Are Integral

A second aspect of excellence in story development involves valuing contributions from the public as central to storytelling, not secondary. Journalists have long relied on eyewitness accounts and public reaction as they have told stories, but in online journalism public accounts and reaction often take a larger place—alongside the contributions of journalists or even sometimes in place of them.

Elizabeth Chuck, social media and breaking news editor for msnbc.com, points to the value that UGC can add to news coverage.

Photo 5.1   Elizabeth Chuck, social media and breaking news editor for msnbc.com, points out that public contributions can expand the reach of news organizations' coverage.

After singer Michael Jackson died, she spent part of her time updating a gallery of photos that users had sent from memorials around the world. (The gallery is no longer on the site.) Reflecting on what the photos as UGC contributed to the storytelling, Chuck says:

> The advantage to showing UGC is that our audience is always places that we're not going to be. We have correspondents and journalists around the world, but they're not necessarily taking pictures of those Michael Jackson memorials. They're not necessarily there, and they're not able to give these first-person accounts of what it's like to be there. So, I think that, just in terms of being able to offer a wider range of coverage—even if it's with the understanding that it's not coming from a professional, that it's coming from someone who's experiencing it as a real, normal person—it expands the reach of where our coverage is coming from.

Sometimes, then, members of the public who are present can provide images that journalists cannot and advance knowledge of the story. Excellence in journalistic practice online means making the most of what members of the public know.

Public contributions have gained a great deal of attention in the past several years in coverage of a number of other high-profile stories. A look at several of these shows the evolution of news organizations' interest in them and use of them, as well as the evolution of the tools that power them including camera phones and social media.

London terrorist bombings, 2005

On July 7, 2005, four suicide bombers launched attacks that killed 52 people and injured hundreds more in London, England. The day of the attacks, cell phones "turned members of the public into reporters and camera crews," as a BBC story put it (Douglas, 2005). Gripping images, both still photos and video, showed blurry scenes from inside the subway. ("Video of Survivors' Accounts," 2008, includes both still and video images.) One photo from the phone of a trapped passenger (BBC News, n.d.) showed the door of the crowded subway car pried open to help clear smoky air (Noguchi, 2005).

Within an hour of the first bomb, the BBC received 50 pictures from the public. "By the weekend it had 1,000 images and dozens of video clips sent by e-mail and direct from mobile phones" (Douglas, 2005). Images from the public showed up on television and on websites across the world.

Screenshot 5.1   This photo from the phone of a passenger trapped in a subway car, shown on the BBC's website, helped to tell the story of the London bombings in 2005. It is an early example of the power of images from members of the public during a developing story.

The images added greatly to the telling of the story because members of the public could be where journalists could not, unless they happened to be in the subway themselves. They enabled both journalists and others to gain a deeper sense of the atmosphere underground and consequently the impact of the attacks on the people who were in the middle of them. Public contributions also added images to some news organizations' work as the story developed later. When suspects were arrested, members of the public were ready with phones or DV cameras to capture images of the arrests (Douglas, 2005).

Virginia Tech shootings, 2007

On April 16, 2007, a gunman killed 32 students and faculty members before killing himself on the campus of Virginia Tech. This time, cell phone images helped to tell the story again, but social media including Facebook also played a huge role.

Jamal Albarghouti, a Virginia Tech graduate student, captured video on his cell phone with sounds of gunfire and images of police rushing to Norris Hall, site of the second round of shooting. He submitted his video to CNN's iReport site for user-generated contributions ("Student Shot Video," 2007). As with the London subway images from people's phones, his video captured a dramatic segment of the developing story that journalists were not on hand to see. And cell phone video from others went up on Flickr and YouTube (Stabe, 2007).

Some students posted on blogs, but they also took advantage of newer means to share information including MySpace and Facebook (Stabe, 2007). A blog tracking the use of social media and searching had this to say later in the day of the shootings:

> Students are using Facebook as a way to share information about students hit, the delayed response of campus officials, misinformation reported by FOX news, and the identity of the shooter. As such, social media sites have become a visible first source of information for journalists. You can see journalists from CBC, NPR, NBC, and more reaching out to students in the comments fields of posts and in Facebook forums. (Zimmermann, 2007)

Thanks to social media, students were able to bypass mainstream media coverage and find out from one another what was happening— and to mourn. But journalists' efforts to work through them on Facebook to develop stories created some resentment (Stabe, 2007). Journalists' experiences trying to develop stories through sensitive students via social media highlighted the need to exercise care in making connections for stories that way.

Iranian election protests, 2009

In June 2009, a disputed presidential election in Iran brought protesters into the streets in a bold challenge to the Islamic Shiite regime (Iran, 2009). The world saw and heard much of this story through text and video communicated first through social media— Facebook and YouTube but particularly this time Twitter. As an article on NYTimes.com put it a few days after the election:

> On Twitter, reports and links to photos from a peaceful mass march through Tehran on Monday, along with accounts of street fighting and casualties around the country, have become the most popular topic on the service worldwide, according to Twitter's published statistics. (Stone & Cohen, 2009)

The number of journalists who could report independently inside Iran was small, and the government was determined to suppress reports from witnesses. Twitter proved to be an ideal tool for protesters because they could push out messages quickly in the 140-character format.

As with the Virginia Tech shootings, many people learned details directly from witnesses or others nearby using social media and bypassing professional journalists. But while the situation in Blacksburg, Virginia, became clearer as journalists did their own reporting, the situation in Tehran remained murky because so few journalists could be on the scene. As a result, fragments of information from social media remained central as journalists tried to develop the story and present it to their readers. (The boxed feature "Striking a Balance" later in this chapter looks at how the *Times* news blog The Lede handled public contributions from Iran in this situation, in which verification was extremely difficult.)

It was clear by 2009 that technology such as cell phone cameras and social media in the hands of citizens could bring powerful added perspective to stories developing both in the United States and internationally. Thoughtful journalists showed excellence in using public contributions to flesh out details, angles, and reactions in reporting. At their best, these contributions multiply the opportunities for eyewitness accounts. That reality was also evident in the coverage of the crash landing of the jet in the Hudson River, as discussed in Chapter 3.

Critical Eye, Respect for the Public

In their book *The Elements of Journalism,* Kovach and Rosenstiel (2007) placed "the discipline of verification" at the heart of journalism. It is, they argued, "what separates journalism from entertainment, propaganda, fiction, or art" (p. 79). Developing stories from London, Blacksburg, and Tehran—and thousands of other stories across the world—are filled with complexities and uncertainty. It is hard for journalists to verify conflicting accounts and details, and speculation is difficult to sort through. Even beyond the breaking news phase, events and their causes can prove hard to understand. Now that journalists have access to a much larger number of public contributions, they have more sources to learn from or share as independent perspectives. But the need to verify does not go away because important stories still create a need for reliable information. The need to verify, combined with the potential benefit of public contributions, points to a third element of excellence in online story development: maintaining a critical eye on user contributions while also respecting the sophistication of the public. In the common terminology of journalistic tradition, that critical eye is editorial judgment.

Apart from the normal difficulties in verification, content submitted electronically poses problems because it is so easy for people to copy and digitally manipulate images and hard to track sources of words and images clearly. Failure to critically evaluate user contributions can have high stakes, apart from the cost in credibility to news organizations. CNN's iReport site, the same place where a worldwide audience saw cell phone video from the scene of Virginia Tech in 2007, distributed a false report in October 2008:

> Steve Jobs was rushed to the ER just a few hours ago after suffering a major heart attack. I have an insider who tells me that paramedics were called after Steve claimed to be suffering from severe chest pains and shortness of breath. My source has opted to remain anonymous, but he is quite reliable. I haven't seen anything about this anywhere else yet, and as of right now, I have no further information, so I thought this would be a good place to start. If anyone else has more information, please share it. (Quoted in Krazit, 2008)

Apple, which confirmed that the report was false, saw its stock drop as much as 5.4% on the day of the posting. Losses in the first hour of trading reduced the company's market value by at least $4.8 billion, though the denial helped shares to recover ("Steve Jobs Suffering Nutritional Ailment," 2009). The U.S. Securities and Exchange Commission took the matter seriously enough to investigate.

CNN said this on the site:

> iReport.com is an entirely user-generated site where the content is determined by the community. Content that does not comply with Community Guidelines will be removed. After the content in question was uploaded to iReport.com, the community brought it to our attention. Based on our Terms of Use that govern user behavior on iReport.com, the fraudulent content was removed from the site and the user's account was disabled. (Quoted in Kafka, 2008)

CNN made clear that this site operated differently from CNN proper, but this embarrassing mistake on something that could have been checked highlights the tension between welcoming user content as a news organization and questioning it. The long-held standards of journalism would call for checking, but that stands in tension with letting users freely contribute. CNN now flags content on the site that it has vetted to distinguish it from what it has not.

For some stories, numerous public contributions may be available but may be difficult or impossible to verify. The shootings in November 2009 at Fort Hood, Texas, that killed 13 people are an example because in the early stage of the story, the fort was locked down. In that case, social media added to reporting, but the focus in news organizations' best early use of social media was on material from journalists and official sources. (The on-the-job profile at the end of this chapter shows how the social media editor at the web operation of the *Austin American-Statesman* used a Twitter feed to help tell the story both as it broke and in the following days.)

Covering the Iranian election protests presented days' worth of challenges to reporters and editors trying to verify what was happening and piece together the bigger picture. The *Times* reflected the difficulty in a story of its own about the decision by it and other news organizations including *The Huffington Post* and *The Guardian* in London to use blogs to present outside contributions including videos and tweets (Stelter, 2009). The headline: "Journalism Rules Are Bent in News Coverage From Iran."

STRIKING A BALANCE: SIFTING ACCOUNTS OF IRANIAN PROTESTS

The coverage of the Iranian election protests on the *Times'* news blog The Lede offers an interesting window on the ethical dilemma of how to use potentially powerful public contributions in a story where it may be difficult or impossible to follow conventional journalistic standards of verification.

The blog tracks top stories on a given day using a combination of material from *Times* journalists, other media sources, and readers as presented by reporter Robert Mackey. On June 22, 2009, 10 days after the election, the blog was filled with posts about the protests and related news as the story continued to develop. The top of the blog said the purpose was to "supplement reporting by *New York Times* journalists inside Iran" (Mackey, 2009).

Much of that supplementing came through social media. For example, this post introduces a video:

Update | 2:06 p.m. A reader sends us a link to this video, which was uploaded to YouTube today, and is said to show Iranian security forces near Haft-e-Tehran Square massing and then confronting protesters on Monday.

The wording makes clear how the *Times* blog got the video, and it hedges the description of its content by saying it "is said to show" security forces facing off against protesters.

(Continued)

(Continued)

Another post drew on an Iranian blogger as a source, a blogger who had in turn used a Twitter-related site to post a photo. Again the wording is hedged to say "what he says" the photo shows.

Update | 11:10 a.m. An Iranian blogger has uploaded to TwitPic what he says is a photograph of the grave of Neda Agha-Soltan, a young woman who was shot and killed on Saturday in Tehran. As we've reported over the past two days, the graphic video of the woman identified as Ms. Agha-Soltan, bleeding and in agony after being shot, has circulated widely online in the past 48 hours.
The photograph carries the caption: "NEDA sleep here."

Another post to The Lede included details from a Twitter feed but also from reporting attributed to news agencies.

Update | 10:58 a.m. A Twitter feed attributed to Mojtaba Samienejad, an Iranian blogger who has been detained in the past, reported about 20 minutes ago that a memorial for those killed on Saturday, including Neda Agha-Soltan, did take place on Monday in Tehran:

Conflict in Hafte Tir Sq between people and Basij and police

People are gathered for Neda Agha Soltan's mourning / in Hftetir SQ

in all buildings in Hafte Tir , Poice with gun are staying

Reuters reported earlier that about 1,000 people had gathered in Tehran, possibly for this memorial. According to a later brief report from A.P., police used tear gas and shots fired in the air to disperse protesters.

In this case, then, the blog used wire coverage to corroborate the tweets attributed to an Iranian source. For another piece of the day's news, Mackey directly solicited help from readers, then used it to confirm a detail of geography.

Update | 3:25 p.m. Thanks to all the other readers who wrote in to help us understand where in Tehran the video we embedded in our 2:06 p.m. update was shot. It is clear that the Sharoudi Sports

Complex, shown in the video, is very close to Haf-e-Tir Square, where an opposition rally was broken up on Monday. We have added a Google map to the 2:06 p.m. update below to give a better sense of the geography.

With this interaction, the *Times* was also able to add a map—again, not its own—showing the proper location.

By another assessment on the *Times'* own site, this kind of reporting "bent" the rules of journalism (Stelter, 2009). Did it bend them too far?

From the standpoint of deontological, or duty-based, ethics, the decision involves considering ethical responsibilities that may be relevant, such as the four from the Society of Professional Journalists code of ethics: seeking truth, minimizing harm, acting independently, and being accountable (Society of Professional Journalists, 1996).

- The blog went farther out on a limb with truth than normal reporting by posting material that is unconfirmed, so it is possible that some of the video or tweets were not true. But Mackey used attribution and qualified wording to make clear to readers when they were not verified. He also sought truth by asking readers to help confirm the location of the video posted at 2:06.

- Minimizing harm is difficult to sort out in this case. It is possible that by helping to alert the world further with the carefully presented information about the plight of protesters, the blog may have helped rally public and government opposition in countries outside Iran. But that is difficult to determine because so much of the story was spreading by social media independent of news organizations.

- The *Times* was acting independently by not simply taking video and text from contributors uncritically but trying to make clear what was confirmed and unconfirmed and using multiple sources to try to corroborate the facts.

- The Lede showed accountability to the public by acknowledging clearly where information was coming from.

From the perspective of virtue ethics:

- The details of this coverage on The Lede show initiative to go beyond traditional journalistic sources but not to go too far and

(Continued)

(Continued)

> embrace them without questioning. The kind of initiative shown represents a mean, in Aristotle's thinking, between deficiency and excess.[1] The appeal to readers for verification shows initiative to try to make sure things are right.
>
> - The honesty that Mackey showed about what is known and unknown also supports this decision from a virtue perspective.
>
> - And on a story that played out over many days, with many fragments of unconfirmed information, sticking to a careful presentation and dialogue with the audience showed perseverance.

User contributions can create a number of pitfalls for online operations, legal as well as ethical. So editorial judgment is essential not only to maintaining journalistic quality but also to avoiding legal fallout. (This discussion does not provide a complete legal overview but touches on two key issues for online journalists. For more information, see the Citizen Media Law Project website, www.citmedialaw.org.)

Online journalists are subject to legal action for libel if they make false and damaging statements in their own work on the sites. But when it comes to contributions from users, they have greater legal protection. Section 230 of the Communications Decency Act (1996) provides broad immunity from liability for third-party material. The immunity remains even if someone at an online site, including a blog or forum, edits this content as long as the editing does not substantially change the meaning. Editing that makes the content defamatory does make the editor responsible, and the legal protection does not apply to any commentary the editor adds to the UGC ("Publishing the Statements and Content of Others," 2009).

UGC can also create problems with copyright for online news sites. But again, federal law provides some protection. Section 512 of the Digital Millennium Copyright Act (1998) provides "safe harbor" provisions against copyright infringement, one of which involves user-contributed creative materials such as photos or audio files. The law provides for protection from liability if the site has effective "notice-and-takedown" procedures, did not know the material was infringing,

---

[1]See Patterson & Wilkins (2008), for a discussion of Aristotle's Golden Mean and its relationship to journalism.

and removes it quickly when a copyright owner gives notice of the infringement ("Protecting Yourself Against Copyright Claims Based on User Content," 2009).

Online journalists have to stay alert to the possibility that users may have lifted content from other sites simply because it is so easy to do. Elizabeth Chuck described an incident at msnbc.com that points up this danger:

> We did have a situation where we got a photo sent in that turned out to be a blatant rip-off from another site, and the user had literally cropped out the copyright from the bottom of the photo, and I think that this is something that sites across the country that are getting user-generated content will have to check for.

Apart from legal concerns, there may be other concerns to think about related to the motives of the person posting the material. Chuck recalled another photo she encountered during the Democratic presidential primary campaign in 2007. Her organization had asked users to send in photos they had taken of candidates. They received one beautiful photo from an Obama campaign event.

> It was Obama, you could see his head and he was smiling and he was reaching out to a crowd of supporters, and there were all these hands— white hands, African American hands—all these arms reaching out to him, and somewhere in the back of the photo in the background there was a supporter holding up a sign that said "Hope."

The photo was so good that she looked up the contributor online and found a site about his work as a freelance journalist. She said that created an ethical dilemma for her. Her questioning led to managers' decision not to use the photo to avoid providing a platform for advertising.

For large sites, the sheer volume of contributions related to news events can be difficult to manage. Tom Brew, deputy editor for distribution at msnbc.com, said one solicitation of user contributions during the presidential election campaign brought about 6,000 responses.

Given all of these difficulties, it is impossible to maintain a standard of excellence in online story development without a critical perspective on user contributions. But at the same time, making the most of what the public can contribute implies an attitude of respect for people's sophistication and ability. Rex Sorgatz, who was executive producer for msnbc.com before leaving to work independently, put his perspective bluntly:

> The public isn't as dumb as we think, as ethics people like to think they are. When I click on a link on a news site and I go to something that has a purple and green header and has 80-point type and is screaming at you, people are knowledgeable enough and have enough media savvy. . . . They understand that I'm now in a different environment—that the information is disputable, too. . . . People who like to point at Wikipedia and say that information is invalid or is potentially invalid are people who are implicitly being condescending to the public, who also understand the same thing that they do. When you're reading those kinds of things you go into it understanding where it's coming from, and so I think that the public is more smart about how this works than people think they are.

Making the most of the open-ended capacity of online storytelling fundamentally means regarding what the public can contribute as valuable. Underlying this perspective is the kind of attitude Sorgatz argues for, respecting the ability of members of the public themselves to maintain an appropriately skeptical stance toward information that comes to them from nonjournalists. This perspective doesn't fit comfortably with traditional views of journalistic practice that expect journalists to be more skeptical than the general public and that call the work of nonjournalists into question.

❖ THE DYNAMIC OF EXCELLENCE

MacIntyre's (2007) theory of a practice again offers a way to step back and look at the impact, real and potential, of developing standards of excellence. The elements of open-ended journalism described in this chapter promise to achieve internal goods and reshape the standard of excellence in the practice of journalism. But it is important to consider this potential with a careful understanding of the place of the public in this view of journalistic excellence. In the pursuit of a standard of excellence that acknowledges the open-endedness of online story development, the maximum potential for achieving excellence comes only if both a critical eye and respect for the public are maintained.

That is a hard balance to achieve. Lurking in the background of online journalism is an ongoing tension between traditional views of reporting information that put the journalist at the center and a fully "open-source" perspective followed by sites such as Wikipedia and its journalistic offshoot, Wikinews. Wiki approaches put users at the center and rely on them to produce and edit content. Many journalists are highly skeptical of the accuracy of information reported on Wikipedia (Shaw, 2008). Wikipedia itself acknowledges the limitations of its accuracy: "It is in the nature of an ever-changing work like Wikipedia that, while some articles are of the highest quality of scholarship, others are admittedly complete rubbish" ("Wikipedia: Ten Things You May Not Know," 2010).

A careful articulation of standards of online journalism is sensitive to the traditions of the broader practice of journalism but also to the central role of the public. This nuanced perspective means not going all the way to reliance on public contributions, as Wikipedia does, but also embracing the value of public contributions and the intelligence of the public. In MacIntyre's (2007) perspective, though, there remains a distinction between the journalist evaluating and using public contributions and the contributor who may follow journalistic standards but may or may not have fully embraced them. It may sound unduly rigid in the open age of the Internet to say, as he does, that anyone who enters a practice must "accept the authority" of the historically developed standards of a practice (p. 190). But acknowledging and reflecting on those standards is essential to maintaining a foundation on which the practice at its best can advance.

In the dynamic MacIntyre describes, pursuing excellence in open-ended story development should lead to achievement of some of the same internal goods of journalism examined in previous chapters. As discussed before, Sandra Borden (2007) pointed out that journalism as a practice involves several internal goods that are common to other intellectual practices such as science: discovery, knowledge, inquiry, originality, and newness. Her discussion of the civic dimension of journalism implies a further good: fostering community. The previous two chapters focused on newness, knowledge, and inquiry. For breaking news, newness is central. Online journalists at their best move fast enough to turn out multiple stories in a day or less in multiple forms, pursuing accuracy and depth, and so enhance the standard of excellence for immediate reporting. They also provide nuanced knowledge built on careful inquiry. In pursuit of comprehensive storytelling online (particularly in larger projects), journalists have the opportunity to elevate the audience's knowledge because they offer more information and, at their best, it is closer to original sources than in reporting for old media. Individual audience members stand to gain knowledge because forms can be chosen according to the story and audience. Use of primary sources and interactivity fosters inquiry.

In this ideal, work that makes the most of the open-endedness of story development also has the potential to achieve particular internal goods. The potential impact becomes clearer if it is viewed in light of the three elements of excellence examined.

• Developing stories in multiple stages in line with their life span advances audience members' knowledge. They have the opportunity to learn information appropriate to their needs and interests at these stages. Building out a story for its full life span provides knowledge that is more enduring than from short-term coverage.

• Treating public contributions as integral to storytelling, not peripheral, may also enhance knowledge because members of the public may be in places where journalists are not. This enhancement of knowledge also adds to the discovery of new insight and perspective about events, particularly as stories are built out with additional contributions over time. Valuing these contributions also furthers inquiry by engaging the public in planning its own role in inquiry related to the story. This engagement may also help foster a sense of community, an issue that will be discussed more in the next chapter focusing on conversation.

• Maintaining a critical eye combined with respecting the ability of the public helps to ensure that accurate knowledge is actually gained. At the same time, it encourages inquiry and may even foster community through appreciation and connection with the public. A key to achieving the balance between a critical eye and respect for the public may lie with an understanding of the role of originality. Borden referred to originality "in the sense of doing your own investigation and thinking" (2007, p. 63). This understanding of originality implies that a journalist must maintain a critical stance in evaluating all information and think beyond what any one source may contribute, with an effort to search out the truth independently. This kind of original work, which is at the bedrock of the best investigative reporting historically, also means that the journalist should never exchange reporting initiative for reliance on others, members of the public or otherwise. Taken together, this understanding of originality suggests that pursuing excellence in the open-ended world of online storytelling maintains a place for the journalist as a critical evaluator of content.

As journalists strive for these dimensions of excellence in storytelling, they uphold the best historical standards of the practice but reshape ideas about excellent storytelling toward a more multistage view of a story's life span and a critical but open stance toward public contributions.

❖ CHALLENGES TO EXCELLENCE IN STORY DEVELOPMENT: EXTERNAL GOODS LURKING

The past two chapters looked at challenges to journalists' ability to achieve speed and accuracy with depth in breaking news and, more generally, comprehensiveness in content. Some of those challenges relate to the medium itself. The capacity of the Internet to accommodate numerous changes and updates creates pressures of expectation, whether from management or the audience or journalists themselves. The capacity for using multiple forms of storytelling with multiple paths stretches the ability of journalists to create packages that are coherent for everyone looking at them. Similarly, focusing on the development of a story in its full life span over time, it becomes clear that the nature of the medium creates opportunities to provide numerous stages of content—but that capacity again implies high expectations and difficulties in clarity of presentation.

Again, though, the nature of the medium is not the only source of challenge to journalists trying to do excellent work online. Some of the pressures relate to what MacIntyre (2007) called external goods. These pressures were more implied than stated in the comments of the journalists interviewed, but they are important to examine to provide a broader context for understanding their work.

One pressure involves quality control of UGC. This chapter has looked at some of the difficulties journalists have to watch for: promotion of individuals with possible commercial interests, lifting content directly from other sources, and verifying the truth of information. Then there is, as Tom Brew at msnbc.com points out, the challenge of sheer volume. Part of the difficulty in monitoring the quality of this content is being sensitive to the ethical and legal ramifications. But a key part of the problem is limitations on staffing. No news organization can deploy unlimited resources, especially in the economic climate of the early 21st century, but the pressure of the external good of profit in these profit-making institutions does constrain their ability to maintain high standards in the evaluation of user contributions. It is impossible to provide a magic formula for how organizations can monitor public contributions better with tight staffs. In fact, the core of the answer lies with the choices of journalists to persevere and conscientiously focus on every task they juggle with great care—to exercise virtue and keep embracing the highest historical standards of the practice.

Another pressure is tied to something else discussed earlier in this chapter: the need to maintain equilibrium between having a critical eye on audience contributions and respecting what the public contributes. The journalists who talked about user contributions showed respect toward the ability of the public to add worthwhile insight to stories. But the more central the place of public contributions becomes, the more it may threaten the distinctive place of journalists. It could prove dangerous to society, no matter how unpopular journalists may be, if news organizations push them aside and rely heavily on public contributions rather than their systematic newsgathering. Unpaid citizens left to fill in the gaps may provide excellent information at times, but there will be a danger of stories not covered or done superficially, or only covered in certain cities. However, if journalists seek to protect their place uncritically, at the expense of careful consideration of what the public can contribute, they may reflect the external good of status rather than internal goods such as knowledge and discovery.

Sorgatz, who left the mainstream outlet of msnbc.com after the interview for this book to pursue independent blogging and consulting, didn't talk in the language of internal and external goods—but, as his comments earlier in this chapter show, he spoke critically about doubting the public's wisdom. ("The public isn't as dumb as we think, as ethics people like to think they are.") His comments are a good reminder that respect for the public takes a central place in the developing practice of journalism in the early 21st century.

❖ ATTITUDE CHECK: VIRTUES FOR 21ST-CENTURY JOURNALISTS

What virtues will help journalists in this environment pursue excellence? Again, the answer lies mostly in the background of the interviews and discussion of what they mean—since journalists don't tend to speak in the language of virtue any more than they dress like virtuous superheroes. Six virtues come to mind:

- **Honesty.** Journalists developing stories in a way that fully integrates public contributions with their own must be honest about the sources of their stories. Part of this involves standard practices of clearly attributing information in articles and accompanying elements that journalists write, just as they do in newspaper or (ideally) in television. It also means clearly identifying what members of the public have contributed so that the audience itself can critically evaluate those contributions.

- **Humility.** The turn in story presentation toward use of public contributions calls for humble recognition on the part of journalists that their knowledge and vantage point in storytelling are limited. Simply using public contributions in an ongoing story implies humility, but humility involves inward attitude as well as outward activity.

- **Perseverance.** As discussed in the chapter on breaking news, this is a key virtue in pursuing stories in their early stages at a high level of quality. Developing a story in the longer term over its full life span also takes perseverance. The critical eye on public contributions also involves persevering to continue adequate monitoring of them over the life of the story, especially after the initial period of intense focus where these contributions may get higher scrutiny in the newsroom. The fact that content lives on potentially indefinitely online makes perseverance in monitoring it particularly important.

- **Initiative.** This virtue is important for journalists who have to seek out public contributions and also exercise careful judgment as they sift through them during developing stories. Robert Quigley, profiled below, showed this kind of initiative in Fort Hood shootings coverage using Twitter.

- **Flexibility.** This is necessary to handle the unpredictable directions in story development, with a wide range of possible content coming from both reporters and the public.

- **Creativity.** The best story development online means thinking of creative ways to blend public and journalist contributions and the forms in which they may arrive.

The next chapter will look at user contributions as part of a broader discussion of the central place of conversation in online journalism.

❖ ON-THE-JOB PROFILE: ROBERT QUIGLEY FACING THE DAILY CHALLENGES

Robert Quigley's title at the *Austin American-Statesman*, social media editor, is a sign of the times as news organizations rethink the ways they

Photo 5.2   Robert Quigley, social media editor at the *Austin American-Statesman*, used Twitter aggressively to report on the developing story of shootings at Fort Hood, Texas, but he also exercised careful judgment to separate speculation from fact.

develop and present stories. The importance of his role became clear on November 5, 2009, after a shooting rampage at Fort Hood, Texas, that left 13 people dead and more than two dozen others wounded. His use of Twitter that day and in the following weeks shows how that tool can help news organizations assemble and communicate important pieces of a developing story.

The questions and answers below are compiled from e-mails in February 2010. They offer insight on how he handled the story, the ethical care he took, and the background and qualities he brings to his job.

What are your responsibilities?

As the social media editor at the *Austin American-Statesman*, I'm charged with making our newsroom staff more, well, sociable. Up until a few years ago, journalists operated on a one-way street. We told people the news without listening to much feedback, and without responding to the community. Social media has changed that. I look for new ways to facilitate that exchange through staff training, by experimenting with new tools and by helping come up with new strategies. I'm also the voice behind the main *Statesman* Twitter account and our Facebook page.

Please walk me through the sequence of events the day of the Fort Hood shootings as you set up and developed the Twitter feed.

As part of my job, I monitor what others are saying on Twitter, including our competition. That afternoon, I saw a tweet from a local TV station saying there were unconfirmed reports that there was a gunman shooting people at Fort Hood. I retweeted the station's post, with proper attribution, and said, "We are working to confirm." Within a few minutes, we had confirmation, and the newsroom swung into action. The *Statesman*'s editor, Fred Zipp, suggested to me that we start an account just for the Fort Hood shootings, and I agreed it would be a good idea. In 2008 during Hurricane Ike, we had set up an account just for our hurricane coverage as the storm pushed through Houston, and that account was a huge success. I created the @FTHoodShootings account [http://twitter.com/FtHoodShootings] in a few minutes, put the *Statesman*'s logo on the account and began tweeting the news as it came in. I used the *Statesman*'s main account, which had more than 17,000 followers at the time, to let people know we had created the new account. Within a few hours, we had more than 3,000 followers on the new account, and it had been put into "Twitter lists" by several of the nation's leading media outlets, including *The New York Times, Huffington Post* and CNN. I was getting updates as they were happening from our reporters at Fort Hood (funneled via phone to an assignments editor) and from other sources, including tweets from the Killeen daily paper and wire stories from the AP. I posted everything newsworthy that I could verify on the account, and ended up posting about 130 tweets in about 6 hours. We posted an automatic widget on our home page [http://www.statesman.com] to show off the tweets to the non-Twitter audience.

What did your job look like as you continued the feed in the days immediately after the shootings? What have you had to do with it since then?

I continued to post updates pretty steadily for the few days after the shootings. After the breaking news fully subsided, I came back and updated with major events, including the medical status of the suspect, the funerals for the soldiers, developments in the investigation. Naturally, the pace of the updates went down.

What were the challenges—technical, practical, ethical if any— in making the feed work initially? And how did you overcome them?

Technically, it was not a problem. We have been using Twitter regularly and aggressively in our newsroom since June 2008, so we were prepared to use the medium. The main difficulty we ran into was that our reporters who were initially sent to the scene didn't have smart phones, so they couldn't post updates themselves. It was a minor inconvenience, though, as we were able to relay what they were telling our desk on the phone into blog posts and tweets. Ethically, I'm very careful to avoid posting any speculation. As I scoured the social media sites looking for news, I did see a lot of rumors and speculation floating around. People turn to the *Statesman* to tell them what's really happening, so I work hard to be sure that what I'm telling them is properly attributed and true to the best of our knowledge.

What do you think the feed has contributed to the telling of this story?

I know that a lot of military members and their family were following our Twitter feed so they could find out what was going on in the immediate aftermath of the shootings. Giving them the facts as they were happening was valuable. Obviously, there was interest beyond those immediately affected as well. We're in the business of telling people what is going on. Tools such as Twitter just make us more effective and timely, if used correctly.

What did you get from contributions from the public that you didn't get from professional news organizations (yours or others)?

In general, contributions from the public are important because although we have the largest newsgathering operation in Central Texas, we cannot be everywhere. For many news events, we rely on public input to tell a more-complete story (getting reader reports during an ice storm would be a good example). In this instance, our reporters and the other professional news outlets had the story. There wasn't a lot of information coming out of the public, and Fort Hood was locked down. I saw tweets from people inside the post saying that all they knew about what was going on was based on what they were seeing from the media outlets.
[An exception:

RT @PrettyBoySlimm: Waiting for word that all is clear so we can get the hell off post and get somewhere we can actually place phone calls! 2:23 PM Nov 5th, 2009 from Seesmic

Quigley: It was a tweet that gave information (the lockdown was still ongoing and phone lines were down). It also didn't include speculation of any kind that would require verification on our side. It wasn't the biggest news item tweeted that day, but it provided a quick glimpse inside the Army post.]

What other responsibilities did you have to juggle with this one initially and later?

As always, we have a responsibility to carefully attribute information, no matter the medium. I wanted to be sure that we were not jumping off the diving board into speculation. Later, I had to be sure that we treated the suspect the same way we treat all people suspected of crimes. Journalistic integrity is important, whether you're publishing on Twitter or in print.

Over the longer term, including later developments, what do you think having this feed available contributes to telling the story?

There is an increasing number of people who get their news solely through social media. People who are still following that feed are likely intensely interested in the turns in the investigation, and we should provide what we know.

What background do you have that prepared you for this job?

Running the Twitter feed and our Facebook page sounds like an easy job—until you realize that I'm speaking on behalf of the entire metro daily newspaper without a copy editor or a manager as a safety net. It takes a feel for news judgment, restraint, an understanding of ethics and good headline writing skills (each tweet ought to be a catchy headline if you want to draw people in). I started as a sports writer at the *Nacogdoches Daily Sentinel*, but I've been an editor for most of my career. Since I've been in Austin (now more than 10 years), I've been a copy editor, page designer, the assistant news editor, letters editor, Internet editor and now social media editor. As assistant news editor, I was the "slot" two or three times a week. The slot is basically the person in charge of the entire print product after the upper management goes home for the day. I made thousands of front-page story play calls, headline wording calls, etc. I also actively sought out holes in stories (to plug them, hopefully). Over years of doing that and watching other smart editors do the same, I sharpened my news judgment skills. My copy editing background is just as valuable since I work to make my social media posts interesting, sharp and accurate. As letters editor, I worked with the public every day and had to forge relationships with op-ed columnists and others who were contributing content to our paper. As Internet editor (which is basically a breaking news editor), I learned the Internet operation inside and out. I've always been a tech-oriented type of guy: I created a website for my parents' book store using html in 1994.

What personal qualities does it take to do the job well?

You have to be an extrovert. I go to Social Media Club meetings, tweetups and lunches and coffee with the big local bloggers. I also speak in public a lot about our efforts to students, nonprofit organizations and more. I want people in the community knowing who I am and understanding what we're trying to do. Just working behind a computer all day only goes part of the way toward achieving that goal.

❖ REFERENCES

BBC News. (n.d.). *BBC News*. Retrieved February 21, 2010, from http://news.bbc .co.uk/2/shared/spl/hi/pop_ups/05/in_pictures_enl_1120742501/html/ 1.stm

Borden, S. L. (2007). *Journalism as practice: MacIntyre, virtue ethics and the press*. Burlington, VT: Ashgate.

Communications Decency Act of 1996, 47 U.S.C. § 230 (2008).

Digital Millennium Copyright Act of 1998, 17 U.S.C. § 512 (2009).

Douglas, T. (2005, August 4). Shaping the media with mobiles. *BBC News*. Retrieved February 15, 2010, from http://news.bbc.co.uk/2/hi/uk_news/4745767 .stm

Inauguration central. (2009, January 20). *washingtonpost.com*. Retrieved February 16, 2010, from http://voices.washingtonpost.com/inauguration-central/

Iran. (2009, May 17). *NYTimes.com*. Retrieved May 17, 2010, from http://topics .nytimes.com/top/news/international/countriesandterritories/iran/index .html

Kafka, P. (2008, October 3). SEC investigating fraudulent Steve Jobs heart attack report. *Business Insider*. Retrieved February 16, 2010, from http://www .businessinsider.com/2008/10/cnn-here-s-why-we-yanked-that-steve- jobs-heart-attack-story-aapl-

Kovach, B., & Rosenstiel, T. (2007). *The elements of journalism: What newspeople should know and the public should expect* (Rev. ed.). New York: Three Rivers Press.

Krazit, T. (2008, October 3). Jobs heart attack rumor not true, Apple stock swings. *CNET News.* Retrieved May 17, 2010, from http://news.cnet.com/8301-13579_3-10057521-37.html

MacIntyre, A. (2007). *After virtue* (3rd ed.). Notre Dame, IN: University of Notre Dame Press.

Mackey, R. (2009, June 22). June 22: Updates on Iran's disputed election. *NYTimes.com.* Retrieved February 16, 2010, from http://thelede.blogs.nytimes.com/2009/06/22/latest-updates-on-irans-disputed-election-3/

Noguchi, Y. (2005, July 8). Camera phones lend immediacy to images of disaster. *washingtonpost.com.* Retrieved February 16, 2010, from http://www.washingtonpost.com/wp-dyn/content/article/2005/07/07/AR2005070701522.html

Patterson, P., & Wilkins, L. (2008). *Media ethics: Issues and cases* (6th ed.). New York: McGraw-Hill.

Protecting yourself against copyright claims based on user content. (2009, October 23). *Citizen Media Law Project.* Retrieved February 16, 2010, from http://www.citmedialaw.org/legal-guide/protecting-yourself-against-copyright-claims-based-user-content

Publishing the statements and content of others. (2009, August 25). *Citizen Media Law Project.* Retrieved February 16, 2010, from http://www.citmedialaw.org/legal-guide/publishing-statements-and-content-others

Shaw, D. (2008, February/March). Wikipedia in the newsroom. *American Journalism Review.* Retrieved February 16, 2010, from http://www.ajr.org/article.asp?id=4461

Society of Professional Journalists. (1996). Code of ethics. *Society of Professional Journalists.* Retrieved February 16, 2010, from http://www.spj.org/ethicscode.asp

Stabe, M. (2007, April 17). Fleet street 2.0: Virgina [sic] Tech shooting raises new issues for journalists. *Press Gazette.* Retrieved February 16, 2010, from http://blogs.pressgazette.co.uk/fleetstreet/2007/04/17/virgina-tech-shootings-raises-new-issues-for-journalists/

Stelter, B. (2009, June 28). Journalism rules are bent in news coverage from Iran. *NYTimes.com.* Retrieved February 16, 2010, from http://www.nytimes.com/2009/06/29/business/media/29coverage.html

Steve Jobs suffering nutritional ailment; to remain Apple chief. (2009, January 5). *NYTimes.com.* Retrieved February 16, 2010, from http://www.nytimes.com/2009/01/05/business/worldbusiness/05iht-05apple.19091182.html

Stone, B., & Cohen, N. (2009, June 15). Social networks spread defiance online. *NYTimes.com.* Retrieved February 16, 2010, from http://www.nytimes.com/2009/06/16/world/middleeast/16media.html?_r=4

Student shot video of campus shooting. (2007, April 16). *CNN.com.* Retrieved February 16, 2010, from http://www.cnn.com/2007/US/04/16/vtech.witness/

Video of survivors' accounts. (2008, July 7). *BBC News.* Retrieved February 16, 2010, from http://news.bbc.co.uk/2/hi/uk_news/7493497 .stm

Wikipedia: Ten things you may not know about Wikipedia. (2010, May 15). *Wikipedia.* Retrieved May 17, 2010, from http://en.wikipedia.org/wiki/ Wikipedia:Ten_things_you_may_not_know_about_Wikipedia

Zimmermann, K. (2007, April 16). Virginia Tech shootings: Role of social media & search in journalism (and the suckiness of contextual ads). *Searchviews.* Retrieved February 16, 2010, from http://www.searchviews.com/ index.php/archives/2007/04/virginia-tech-shootings-role-of-social- media-search-in-journalism-and-the-suckiness-of-contextual-ads.php

❖ COMPANION WEBSITE

Visit the companion website at **www.sagepub.com/craigstudy** for links to examples of online journalism.

6

The Centrality of
Conversation

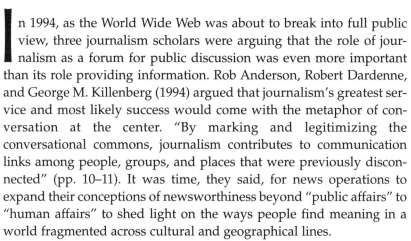

In 1994, as the World Wide Web was about to break into full public view, three journalism scholars were arguing that the role of journalism as a forum for public discussion was even more important than its role providing information. Rob Anderson, Robert Dardenne, and George M. Killenberg (1994) argued that journalism's greatest service and most likely success would come with the metaphor of conversation at the center. "By marking and legitimizing the conversational commons, journalism contributes to communication links among people, groups, and places that were previously disconnected" (pp. 10–11). It was time, they said, for news operations to expand their conceptions of newsworthiness beyond "public affairs" to "human affairs" to shed light on the ways people find meaning in a world fragmented across cultural and geographical lines.

Even though these three authors were not focusing on the Internet, the kind of journalism for which they argued looks startlingly like the journalism—minus clear boundaries—that has developed online in the early 21st century. The names and sites connected with online conversation are changing rapidly, but conversation occupies a more central place than it ever did in print or broadcast media.

This chapter will:

- Put the centrality of conversation online in the context of old and new developments in journalism. The discussion will connect with Sandra Borden's (2007) ideas about the *telos*, or purpose, of journalism and how that purpose may differ from the purposes of conversation in other spheres.

- Describe features of excellence in online conversation, again drawing on thoughts of some of the journalists interviewed and examples from a variety of places. The focus will be on three online forms where conversation is particularly central: blogs, including reader comments and dialogue; discussion forums; and social media.

- Look at the ways that online conversation can further the good of fostering community, as well as knowledge and inquiry, and consider what can stand in the way of that.

- Profile an opinion writer on the job as he writes about politics, showing how he uses his blog to build conversation with and among his readers.

❖ A LONGTIME VALUE TAKES CENTER STAGE

A full intellectual history is beyond the scope of this book, but the idea that fostering conversation should be central to the work of journalism runs back, in the American context, to the founding of the country and the First Amendment's assurances of freedom to express ideas. It has roots in John Milton's argument (2003) and John Stuart Mill's development (2003) of the notion that ideas should be exchanged in a free and open intellectual marketplace, although in practice the marketplace has always been constrained by limitations such as class, race, and gender. The notion of conversation as a key feature of journalism has focused primarily on discussion related to important public issues because this kind of discussion is vital to the functioning of an active democracy. The Hutchins Commission in the 1940s highlighted the priority of mass communication as "a forum for the exchange of comment and criticism" open to "all the important viewpoints and interests in the society" (Commission on Freedom of the Press, 1947, pp. 23–24). As noted in Chapter 2, recent writing such as Kovach and Rosenstiel's *Elements of Journalism* (2007) also points to journalism's role in democracy, opening a place for conversation.

But the print news media have typically presented limited opportunities for conversation between journalists and audience members and among audience members. Adam Najberg, senior editor for video at *The Wall Street Journal*, puts it this way:

> Journalism has been sort of a one-way proposition mostly because that was the way it was and that was the way the media format allowed. The only way you could kind of get readers to respond was through letters to the editor, "vox pop" on the street, and it was mostly because the reporter or the newspaper decided to open up that forum. But the whole discussion was really kind of guided in the first place by the media.

Newspapers have traditionally provided limited vehicles such as letters and interviews of people on the street, and space permitted few people to have a say through those means. And, as Najberg notes, discussion was highly controlled by the organizations. Broadcast operations have more naturally provided means of conversation through on-air discussion involving journalists, program guests, and members of the public present or calling in.

In the 1990s, a few more doors opened in print and broadcast media because of the movement known as civic or public journalism. Efforts under this umbrella were intended to "help revive the flagging vitality of public life by listening systematically to citizens, increasing civic knowledge, citizen participation, issue awareness, reasoned analysis of issues and, thereby, an informed and active electorate." The hope was that the news media outlets would connect better with the public and empower citizens to solve community problems (Lambeth & Craig, 1995, p. 149). Newspapers and broadcast outlets, and later web operations, took on a huge range of projects under this umbrella, sometimes working together. The journalists who led these projects used a variety of techniques unconventional for mainstream journalism such as focus groups of citizens and public forums. Conversation was central to some of these projects such as one at *The*

Photo 6.1   Adam Najberg, senior editor for video at *The Wall Street Journal*, says newspaper journalism has been "a one-way proposition" with a few exceptions such as letters to the editor.

Miami Herald called Community Conversations, in which editors and reporters met with groups of 10 to 12 residents to listen to their concerns. The groups represented a variety of common interests—for example, a homeowners' group, downtown businesspeople, or caregivers. The conversations became background for reporters covering public issues and sometimes made it into publication in edited form. Another project, in Dayton, Ohio, called Kids in Chaos, focused on juvenile violence using a variety of techniques involving dialogue: small-group discussions among citizens about youth crime, a conference with experts on youth violence, interviews with young people, and town forums in which concerned community members talked about solutions. (See Lambeth & Craig, 1995, for more background on these efforts.)

Civic journalism took a beating from many journalists and scholars, partly over concerns that journalists were abandoning their independent judgment about public issues (Black, 1997). Although independence is an important ethical value, as the Society of Professional Journalists' ethics code (1996) underlines, the development of the highly interactive world of online communication has put the public's judgment and engagement in discussion front and center. Anyone thinking about standards of excellence in journalism has to consider the fact that conversation about matters large and small is a key part of what people expect online, and that it does not happen along neatly laid-out boundaries between who is and is not a journalist. Opportunities for conversation online have exploded as the Internet has expanded—from message boards beginning in the 1990s to blogs and social networking sites such as Facebook and Twitter in the following decade. Interested citizens, whether nice or nasty, debate issues with one another and with bloggers. Independent bloggers and community journalists engage people in discussion on politics and a huge range of other topics. Millions of people worldwide use social media to talk about their personal lives and issues of common interest.

Most of this development occurred outside mainstream media outlets, but journalists working for them have joined the fray in many ways—tracking issues, building sources, and engaging in conversation of their own on their organizations' websites and outside. For journalists, though, the lack of boundaries among places of conversation online puts them in a difficult position if they want to distinguish what they do professionally from what others do without withdrawing from important sites of conversation. Online and on television and radio, conversation goes on all the time without clear distinctions among the functions of information, interpretation, opinion, entertainment, and commerce. Bloggers, for example, may present opinions supported by fact or just rant about political opponents. Talk-show hosts may provide information without a full picture of all sides because they're trying to entertain as well as provoke discussion.

In this environment, the distinctive place of journalism does not rest with where the journalist is conversing but rather with the goal, or *telos*, of journalism. In Borden's view, built out of virtue ethics, that *telos* is ultimately "to help citizens know well in the public sphere" (2007, p. 50). This kind of knowledge, communicated as news, allows humans to flourish and promotes the common good. Journalism's commitment to the common good under this view gives it a civic dimension, not just an intellectual dimension. This perspective, then, implies that fostering community is one of the internal goods of journalism—alongside fostering knowledge. Pursuit of community, as well as knowledge, with the goal of helping citizens "know well" should distinguish conversation that goes on in the practice of journalism, whether in small or large news operations and whether the vehicle is a blog, forum, or social media.

Conversation is a key element of fostering community, so it is important to look carefully at how the centrality of conversation in online journalism may help foster community—or hinder it. The next section will discuss standards of excellence in online conversation. The section after that will consider them in light of the good of fostering community, as well as intellectual goods including knowledge and the greater goal of journalism.

❖ STANDARDS OF EXCELLENCE IN ONLINE CONVERSATION

As journalists and news organizations have navigated the online world and adapted to it, some ideas and models for good work have developed, although standards of excellence are not set in stone. The discussion here will continue using thinking and examples from journalists at large news sites, but these ideas are not unique to them—and sometimes they have developed elsewhere first. (Chapter 7 will look at some work from community and independent journalists.) This section will focus on three places where conversation has been particularly prominent: blogs, including reader comments and dialogue; discussion forums; and social media.

Blogs

Characteristics of the blogging form set up the possibility of an abundance of conversation: Bloggers can frequently and directly address readers, and it is easy for readers to add their comments. But the existence of the form does not equate with excellence in fostering conversation. From the standpoint of journalism's role in stimulating conversation, two characteristics of excellent blogs stand out from the interviews. A blog that makes the most of the possibility for conversation:

- Develops a distinct voice and personality.

- Effectively brings readers into a dialogue/conversation.

Develops a distinct voice and personality

Strong blogs often stand out because of the voice they bring to readers—although blogs are also good for doing quick updates of news, a use in which voice and personality are less important than clear information. (Chapters 3 and 5 include examples of blogs used for breaking news.)

Alan Boyle, science editor for msnbc.com, has been doing the Cosmic Log blog since 2002. He said people reading blogs expect a personal element they might not look for in a conventional news story. "You're trying to tell more the context of that story and inject more of your personality into it." In his view, part of excellence in blogging is developing "the person behind the curtain," someone who "becomes your guide to what's important in the world." With his writing on Cosmic Log, Boyle becomes that guide for an audience interested in science. But his voice is a subdued one, authoritative but open to correction and interaction. His posts are packed with information including original reporting, and he states little overt opinion or strong language. He also uses little first person, but the places it shows up include updates in response to discussion or later information. His awareness of the conventions of journalistic practice colors his view of how distinctive his voice should be.

It's certainly something that is more expected and more part of the milieu in the blogging universe. And it's something that maybe I have a hard time with sometimes because I'm from more of a traditional journalism background, and so I feel like I don't need to get up on the soapbox and hold forth or pontificate on something. I've always felt that I had the attitude meter on my blog turned down quite a

bit. . . . I hope that a wider range of people feel comfortable coming to
the blog and interacting.

Boyle, writing on a serious and complex subject, displays a blogger
personality but a quiet one informed by his awareness of the traditions
of journalism as a practice.

Bill Grueskin, who as managing editor for WSJ.com was a driving
force behind the development of blogs there, pointed out that when a
blog has an identifiable voice, it gives people a sense of the world-
view of the person writing (something buried by the objectivity con-
vention of traditional journalistic writing). One popular blog for the
Journal, called The Juggle, looks at issues related to people's struggles
to juggle work and family. Rachel Emma Silverman, a mother of two
young children in Austin, Texas, is editor and cowriter for the blog.
The transparency she shows in writing about concerns of parents
gives readers perspective on who she is. For example, she posted an
entry about a *Washington Post* story about the nightmare of forgetting
a child in the car long enough that the child would get too hot and
die. She wrote this:

> When my son was a newborn and I was in the haze of new momhood,
> I had moments when my heart skipped a beat. I'd be driving and
> couldn't see or hear him, and I would wonder if he was still in the
> car—did I leave him in the restaurant? Or I'd be tempted to leave him
> peacefully sleeping so I could run into a convenience store or into the
> post office, instead of toting around the bulky infant seat.

She ended the post by directly addressing readers with these questions: "Have you had any near-miss moments of parental forgetfulness? How do you view these parents whose infants have died of
hyperthermia?" (Silverman, 2009). The post generated more than 100
comments, showing that it had struck a nerve with readers.

Tim Hanrahan, assistant managing editor for WSJ.com, said that
having one or two people writing consistently for a blog helps to show
"that this is different from just a conglomeration of news bits. . . . When
they are more group efforts they tend to read more like group efforts."

The more personal voice of blogs can make for a more engaging
form of storytelling than a straight news story. Rex Sorgatz, former
executive producer for msnbc.com and a blogger himself, sees the blog
form as a way for a media organization to "supply a more intimate,
personal voice to the new generation." Bloggers can develop a closer

relationship with readers because the interaction with them builds mutual understanding. The closer relationship might appear danger-ous, Sorgatz says, but he sees it as good. To him, blogging fits within the beat reporting tradition of journalism and creates a community of interest around a topic or an entire industry. The more personal approach has roots in the history of the practice of journalism, but it differs from the recent tradition of objective reporting. Sorgatz argues that this approach is more interesting for readers.

> It's more like extending the idea toward a new form of storytelling, a different way to convey information. And they are ultimately much more compelling, because if someone is covering a beat and they're updating it four times a day and you care about that beat, to be able to go back to it four times a day and see two new paragraphs added is just a much more interesting experience than this crafted seven-graph story that appears the next morning. It has no personality to it.

Sorgatz relates the shift to more personal voice to broader devel-opments in media in recent years in which the first-person narrative form has become more dominant. He sees that reflected in reality TV, talk radio, documentary, creating one's own music from previous music, and memoirs in the book industry.

Hal Straus, interactivity and communities editor for washington post.com, offers another historical perspective:

> Certainly in the history of the U.S. press, the standard tone of reports has not been as dry or as objective, I guess as scholarly, as it is today. And I think our media demands a more conversational tone in general.

He points out that communication styles change with time.

> Nobody, for instance, would write about the important issues today in a thesis-counterthesis structure. But yeah, that's the way church debates were conducted in the Middle Ages, and were they wrong? No! But they don't work today. I think in the same way having many of our online features written with voice, written with conversational tone, I just think it's natural.

This long historical perspective underlines the fact that choices about voice and writing style can change as part of broader traditions of culture or profession. In this light, one can see the development of blogs as part of the evolution of the practice of journalism.

Brings readers into dialogue/conversation

Communication of a voice and personality sets the stage for interaction with readers. As Carla Baranauckas, assistant to the editor on the continuous news desk at *The New York Times*, puts it:

> A blog starts from being one person's point of view, and then when you have the comments that come in from a reader it really can turn into a conversation, and that's where I think people want to know that they're speaking to another human being and not speaking to a brick wall.

But excellence in blogging also means going beyond voice and personality to make the most of the opportunity to foster conversation involving the blogger and readers. Structurally, blogs are well suited to conversation because they allow readers to comment on posts and on one another's comments, and the blogger can make further comments. The prospect for interaction, though, is enhanced when the blogger directly asks for feedback. Silverman's (2009) questions on The Juggle about readers' experience and opinions on parents' forgetfulness are a good example.

Screenshot 6.1   Alan Boyle asks readers directly for their opinions on some of the intriguing subjects he writes about on his Cosmic Log science blog.

Another example of asking readers for comments comes from Cosmic Log. In a post in June 2009, Boyle wrote about a book that argued, as he put it, "that our consciousness plays a central role in creating the cosmos." Boyle said the thesis of the book, *Biocentrism*, by Robert Lanza with Bob Berman, was controversial. "Any claim that space and time aren't cold, hard, physical things has to raise an eyebrow," he told his readers. At the end of the post, which included quotes from Lanza and some reflections from Boyle on the topic, he asked for comments directly: "Does all this make a difference in daily life, or how you see the world? Take a look at the free sample of 'Biocentrism,' and feel free to weigh in with your comments below" (Boyle, 2009).

More than 100 readers did weigh in. Boyle talked in an interview about why he solicited comments in that post:

> I'm not the expert, and I think that to give people the impression that I can dictate what the grand answer to a cosmic question is going to be would be a little bit presumptuous on my part. I do feel as if there are so many smart people and thoughtful people out there—and maybe some people who aren't as smart but still have an opinion on this—and so I want to encourage that interplay of opinion.

His comment shows the respect he has for his audience and his desire to foster exchange of ideas on a deep question. He said he pictures the conversation on this sort of issue as the kind people might have with friends around a campfire.

> I think that the web-mediated conversation can go in that direction. Just as somebody discusses the news of the day, somebody can have a place where they discuss those crazy ideas that come to you as you're looking up at the stars.

Boyle's "virtual campfire circle" works partly because he writes about interesting topics that stir people's imaginations. But particularly when those topics are ones without clear answers, he sees added value in asking for comments.

Ashby Jones, editor of the *Journal*'s Law Blog, puts spurring conversation in the context of using the blog to "generate buzz and create a community." He describes a similar approach to generating discussion:

> An easy way to do that is to take a controversial issue, cue up both sides and then throw the question out to the readers rather than

actually answering it ourselves. It doesn't bother me at all if we don't get to opine on a lot of things. I'd rather stay sort of agnostic on that on most of those blog posts.

This approach rests within the journalistic tradition of presenting both sides of a story and not injecting one's own opinion. But it can foster discussion among readers. An example is a post in which Jones talked about a *New York Times* story reporting on a test that two researchers evaluated as a replacement for the LSAT. After describing the study on the predictive power of the test, he closed the post this way:

> LB Readers, we remember thinking, at the ripe old age of 23, that the LSAT was a challenging and fair test. Looking back after law school, our unscientific research told us that folks who did better on the test tended to perform better in the classroom and, we assumed, those were the folks most cut out for a long and successful lawyering career. But maybe we were wrong. Any thoughts? (Jones, 2009)

The post prompted 23 comments—not a huge number but enough to show that it had generated interest to draw a variety of readers into the discussion. Other posts that did not lay out sides of an argument or close with a direct question to readers also prompted discussion, but this kind of setup means the blogger is doing everything possible to invite it—without resorting to inflammatory language.

Bloggers covering politics—one of the major topics of blogs and one of the most important for journalism's public purpose—naturally stir discussion among their readers. When they get involved directly in the conversation themselves, exchanges can get heated but also spur more discussion on issues. The on-the-job profile at the end of this chapter focuses on Eric Zorn, a veteran writer for the *Chicago Tribune* who blogs about Chicago and Illinois politics on the paper's site. His posts sometimes set off lengthy debate, and he doesn't hesitate to jump into the middle of it.

Like blogs, conventional articles can foster discussion. But the conversational approach of many blogs makes them a more natural place for robust discussion that includes the writer. Reader comments, though, have added greatly to the opportunity for audience discussion of stories compared with the situation in newspapers before stories went online. The availability of comment space as a normal part of online stories has helped to further establish the central place of conversation in online journalism.

Discussion Forums

Before blogs caught on, members of the public had been debating issues online via discussion forums. Many of these took place away from journalistic websites, but some news organizations have given them substantial space. The *Post*, for example, has hosted a number of groups on topics including politics, values, education, and jobs (Groups, n.d.). Although both blogs and social media are providing other avenues for online discussion now, part of the development of the practice of journalism toward more conversation has come through forums.

Michael Ross, a former news editor, writer, and producer for msnbc.com, has seen the power of public discussion and its disturbing side as well. He oversaw a race and ethnicity forum on the site that sometimes drew comments in huge numbers, as with a discussion of illegal immigration in 2009 (after he left) that drew 44,950 messages. (Msnbc.com has since shut down its discussion boards and migrated to discussion on Newsvine, a company it acquired.) Ross, a veteran print and online writer and editor, has bridged the era of little or no feedback to news media outlets and the era of discussion involving, at times, vast numbers of people. The interview with him for this book suggests two elements of excellence in management of forums:

- Encourage self-direction among users in participation.
- Monitor discussion but allow self-policing.

Encourage self-direction among users in participation

Ross has developed great respect for the ability of people to carry on discussion on message boards. He has seen all kinds of responses—thoughtful, irrelevant, and unacceptably abusive. But he has been impressed with the initiative of people who really want to talk about an issue. He saw a huge range of comments in 2007 after talk show host Don Imus, whose radio program was simulcast on MSNBC cable, made a racially charged remark about the Rutgers University women's basketball team (Faber, 2007). The board received more than 1 million page views before the discussion with his question and people's responses was taken down. Off-topic responses were appearing and, beyond that, responses that were racially or sexually abusive. But even in this case, Ross was impressed by the initiative people had been showing to ask questions of their own, both before and after he had posted his question.

This is the thing about message boards I find so powerful, that people are utterly self-directed about this kind of thing. They came up with their own questions. They want their own friends on the same topic, and here and there you've got other folk that are jumping into the same topic while they're doing a question that they started rather than waiting for me to do it.

Ross' experience suggests that part of making the most of the potential for discussion on a message board is to let users direct the flow of dialogue as much as possible.

Monitor discussion but allow self-policing

When it comes to monitoring, versus allowing participants to monitor themselves, journalists take a range of viewpoints. Ross said his approach was to try to follow comments as people were putting them on the site.

And the thing that I've found in the time that I've done this . . . is that by and large people are pretty good self-monitors. For the most part, their mama's raised them right in terms of knowing what they can say, knowing how far they can go, how much they can push the proverbial envelope on public behavior.

He has seen that people are willing to step up and challenge others posting on a discussion thread.

There have been times when somebody will clearly be going off the deep end and rather than me having to play schoolteacher, wagon whip, finger in their face, other posters on the thread will say, "Hey, take it to another room or take it to another website. We're trying to have a discussion here back and forth going on, and frankly you're not helping. You want to vent in the discussion, clean up your act or move on."

In his view, the best monitoring means letting discussion play out as much as possible. In terms of journalistic excellence, it might seem odd to praise a practice of leaving people to their own devices with only minimal intervention by a journalist, but that approach communicates respect for members of the public and allows ideas to flow in the freest way possible. Abandoning the monitor role altogether would go too far, allowing extreme and destructive comments to sideline effective interchanges. The role that Ross describes represents a constructive balance.

However, there is a range of workable balances of hands-on and hands-off that respect public discussion and avoid sidetracking it. Eric Zorn, the *Chicago Tribune* columnist profiled at the end of this chapter, takes a more aggressive stance on moderating discussion. He is moderating a political blog called Change of Subject, not a discussion forum, but his perspective is important to the topic. He directly challenges readers to bring their best argument—their "A game"—rather than calling him names. He sometimes blocks future access for people who are rude in their comments, especially if they are rude repeatedly. He said he thinks the reason the tone of discussion on his blog is "somewhat higher here than in less moderated forums" is that "I do push back, and people know they can't just get up and say it and repeat the same old thing." In his view, then, he is fostering a higher quality of discussion by leaving less to people's self-policing.

DECIDING WHEN COMMENTS ARE OVER THE TOP

Whether the format is a blog, discussion forum, or story comments, deciding what is too much is an important matter for news organizations hosting user comments. The issues are partly legal. As Chapter 5 noted, federal law does provide substantial legal immunity for online sites even if they edit the comments, as long as the editing does not substantially alter the meaning. But the editor is responsible for changes that make the content defamatory or for commentary the editor adds ("Publishing the Statements and Content of Others," 2009).

Apart from legal issues, there are ethical choices about what to do with comments that are legal but insulting or distracting from the topic. Eric Zorn, a columnist and political blogger for the *Chicago Tribune*, has to deal with strong comments every day on his blog, Change of Subject. Although the vast majority remain, he may take out a comment or even ban the user from the site by blocking the person's IP address. He has banned users for:

- Calling him a "douche bag" whose column "makes me puke to read."

- Saying, "This column was pure drivel. You are scum."

- Saying, "You columnists should all be fired."

- Calling him "chickenshit" (which got past a word filter).

- Using racist and anti-Semitic language.

He will also delete individual comments he does not think are productive for discussion.

Where is the ethical balance between letting every comment through and taking out too much?

From the perspective of the ethics of duty, three of the principles from the Society of Professional Journalists Code of Ethics (1996) are relevant:

- Seeking truth is part of the goal of discussing public issues. Banning users for milder comments—such as "you columnists should all be fired"—might help to chill someone else's interest in contributing a viewpoint that brings out some truth about a topic. But none of these comments advances understanding of readers.

- Taking out the comments that are racist or anti-Semitic could minimize harm to people in the audience who might be hurt by them. The others are directed mostly at Zorn himself, and in a way more annoying than hurtful.

- Being willing to ban users is, in a sense, being accountable to his larger audience of readers who want to talk about local politics in a thoughtful way.

From the vantage point of virtue ethics:

- Being willing to ban users who don't contribute constructively represents an exercise of courage. But the mean in exercising courage here might fall between banning no one and blocking users frequently and for merely annoying remarks.

- Monitoring the comments, and particularly going through the steps to ban a user, takes initiative. While that kind of initiative might seem to run against the purpose of free conversation, it may help to foster it for those more serious about gaining knowledge.

Social Media

With the explosion of social media, news organizations of various sizes have taken to sites such as Facebook, Twitter, and YouTube to open new venues for conversation about news. What excellence looks like is in development, but simply having a presence and being willing to experiment are important.

The New York Times is a good example of a news organization getting engaged on Facebook (*The New York Times*, 2010). As of early 2010, it had more than 500,000 fans, far more than many other news operations. Its Facebook wall on a February day included summaries of stories on a wide range of topics from the Olympics to a new military offensive in Afghanistan, a Belgian train collision, and how Christian the founders of the United States were. Numbers of comments ranged from fewer than 10 to more than 100. The stories receiving the most comments were about the founders (123), the Afghan offensive (126), and reported charges against a professor in the shooting deaths of three faculty members in Alabama (129). But the largest number on the page (148) came on a direct question about what users thought of the opening ceremony of the Vancouver Winter Olympic Games.

The sharing and individual conversations about stories that go on across the Internet every day go far beyond what organizations may initiate through Facebook or other sites. News organizations themselves enable readers to share stories with others through e-mail and sharing/discussion sites such as Digg. Readers take initiative to share stories themselves, such as through Twitter.

Standards of excellence are clearly under development when it comes to how these organizations harness social media to foster conversation. As social media sites keep rising, falling, and changing, a key part of excellence is simply establishing a presence in as many ways and as many places as possible around what, at its best, is a strong foundation of careful news coverage.

Excellence also means being willing to experiment with new or hybrid approaches. One example of a creative hybrid was msnbc.com's page for the Michael Jackson memorial service in July 2009. The page, mentioned in Chapter 4, placed a Twitter feed next to video from the service, enabling readers to comment as they watched. (See "Live Coverage," n.d., still showing some Twitter feed.) Elizabeth Chuck, social media and breaking news editor for msnbc.com, points out that something is lost when people cannot react and see what others are saying in the moment. This approach enabled users to connect emotionally with what was happening at specific times. It represented a creative attempt at integration of content for conversation.

❖ THE DYNAMIC OF EXCELLENCE IN CONVERSATION

It is important again to anchor the discussion of standards of excellence in the ethical framework from Alasdair MacIntyre's work

(2007). Internal goods are a key concept. The focus on conversation puts fostering community in the spotlight as a good of the practice of journalism because dialogue among the members of communities is essential to construct and maintain them. Do the approaches described in the handling of blogs, discussion forums, and social media help to foster community?

The discussion of blogs earlier in this chapter argued that they make the most of the possibility for conversation when they develop a distinct voice and personality, although some news blogs may serve well in breaking news with multiple reporters and no distinct voice. It stands to reason that by building a more intimate connection with readers than traditional reporters did, bloggers will engage them more fully in the community of interest around which the blog is built. That could be a huge range of things: professional fields such as law or finance, family roles such as parenting, personal interests including science or music, or interests in public issues and politics. Not all of these serve the civic role of journalism, but in all these areas an engaging and knowledgeable blogger can help strengthen interest in a topic and connect people with similar interests, if not similar views.

The chapter also pointed out that blogs build conversation, more obviously, when they effectively bring readers into a dialogue with the blogger and one another. Dialogue, especially when it continues regularly over an extended period, helps people to stay connected with one another and with the blogger. Blogs that work daily to keep people talking and continue for months or years could have a powerful impact on the relevant community. This kind of interaction goes well beyond the mostly one-way communication that characterized old media.

Like blogs, online discussion forums are often built around specific common interests. Those interest areas may constitute communities, too. Forums that encourage self-direction among users and self-policing, balanced with monitoring, provide a strong basis for discussion that is robust and substantive. Groups that leave the users highly empowered put their ability to connect with one another more in their own hands, planting the seeds for fostering community, while monitoring helps keep the worst instincts of some users from dominating and harming community.

Social media sites have been fostering connections among millions of people worldwide, quite apart from what news organizations are doing with them. It remains to be seen how fully journalists will engage with users and users with one another around stories as social media continue to evolve. But the potential for fostering two-way flow between journalists and the public is great given the huge number of people who have become accustomed to using social media daily. Likewise, discussion among users built around journalistic reporting shows great promise to draw in large numbers of people. The depth of community that develops will certainly vary, but journalists who engage their audiences with these tools frequently and creatively have the potential to build common interest in public issues.

Two other internal goods discussed in other chapters, knowledge and inquiry, could also be furthered across a range of interests through blogging, forums, and social media. Public contributors can enhance the knowledge of other members of the public and bloggers or discussion moderators themselves if they bring thoughtful comments to the table based on accurate information. Users can also build the knowledge of reporters and one another through discussion around stories linked to from social media sites. It's clear that not everyone will meet a high standard of thoughtfulness, but some likely will. These forms of interaction also provide a natural means to pursue inquiry. Borden (2007) related the good of inquiry to, in the words of Lorraine Code, "substantiating beliefs and knowledge claims" (Code, 1987, p. 53, as cited in Borden). By this definition, journalists and members of the public can serve as a cross-check on each other by demanding and/or providing evidence in support of beliefs and assertions of fact. This cross-checking represents an enhancement of accountability well beyond what was easily possible in print media or on television.

These online activities, then, at their best, reshape the idea of excellence in journalism. By enhancing the possibilities for interaction around a multiplicity of common interests, they strengthen the capacity of journalism to foster community. By adding to the number of voices discussing both political and other issues, they enhance the ability of journalism to gather information and also to check its accuracy. They hold promise to help to realize the *telos* "to help citizens know well in the public sphere" (Borden, 2007, p. 50).

❖ NOW FOR THE CHALLENGES: STUMBLING BLOCKS IN THE "CONVERSATIONAL COMMONS"

When millions of members of the public take center stage in the world of journalism, things get more complicated even as they get more promising. It would be wildly simplistic to assert that excellence in journalism will jump forward in this highly conversational world without facing some significant challenges, some of them related to external goods that again lurk in the background.

Even the idea of fostering community itself can be double edged, connected to both internal and external goods. This duality is implied in some comments by David Patton, former senior editor at WSJ.com. He talked in 2007 about the value of reader comments in the context of the shift at the time to "web 2.0," emphasizing interaction and involvement with the public.

> In terms of a greater journalism value, I'm not sure if there really is one. I think it's a connection thing, and that's the buzzword now on the web with 2.0 is community. Everybody loves community, and I think that has a lot to do with the idea behind stickiness and repeat business. You know that's really what you want, you want people to feel engaged and you want them to come back and read over and over again.

He elaborated a bit later in the discussion, commenting on the narrow focus of blogs.

> I think that the community issue is that it's useful because people will connect to it on a personal level, and those are the same people who are then going to seek out the same content in other places. I think that you're trying to keep them there as a publisher, and I think with that it works in the same way, that the commentary builds a community around it and will get people to come back and read it and maybe they'll forward it to a friend or something like that. It sounds a little bit like a "businessey" answer, but I think that in reality we all want to be read.

It would be wrong to imply that Patton cynically regarded community as only a means to profit, and his concern for excellence in journalism was evident. But the reality, as he transparently noted, is that an important aspect of the drive to promote community in online journalism has been to draw readers to a site and keep them interested, in furtherance of the business interests of the site. People who gather as a community around a topic are realizing the internal good of fostering community, but they are also serving the external good of profit (or that is the hope). The profit in itself is not bad and may help the site survive, but if profit does not develop then the site may not seek to foster community—which, as an internal good, is integral to journalism as a practice unlike profit. Another concern is that the kinds of communities a site may pursue or choose not to pursue can be distorted by business interests. Fostering community around public issues that help democracy work may be harder at times than building around special interests.

Both may serve the greater good in virtue ethics of human flourishing, but the common good may not be advanced significantly.

A related danger that may connect with external goods involves the choice in blogs between doing original reporting and stating opinions. Kari Huus, a reporter for msnbc.com, voices this worry about blogs:

> I think that they bring the hazards of too much about us and too little about the topic, too much about the reporter and the reporter's opinions. I guess it falls generally into the area of commentary, but it strikes me that there's just so much commentary in the world. I guess the greatest hazard is that it comes in place of really well-researched reporting.

As Huus herself would probably acknowledge, some bloggers—such as Boyle writing about science—do solid original reporting. But her comments go to what Sandra Borden (2007) regarded as the central mission of journalism as practice: reporting. A large part of what bloggers do, even on the news sites this book has focused on, is to report on what others are reporting and add opinions or invite the opinions of others. As this chapter has discussed, the conversation that promotes has value in promoting community and adding to the knowledge of the journalists and members of the public. However, these organizations have a finite amount of resources to devote to journalistic work, and they face great pressures to reduce resources and staff in the economic climate of the early 21st century. Writing and soliciting opinions is cheaper than in-depth reporting, so again the external good of profit lies in the background with the potential to squeeze out some original reporting. It is important in the 21st-century version of journalism as practice to note that the conversation itself often becomes part of the reporting, but the danger that independent investigation by reporters will suffer remains.

Beyond these challenges, others that are less clearly linked to external goods pose difficulties for journalists trying to pursue excellence in fostering conversation. They are connected, in various ways, to the nature of the formats being used and the nature of the public contributing to the conversations.

- Discussions can get out of hand, whether they develop around stories of national interest or local controversies. Contributors may post comments that are irrelevant to the topic or outright abusive. And Hal Straus of washingtonpost.com notes that "conversations potentially can be manipulated by folks with particular agendas" such as supporters of a candidate who might flood the discussion with comments in favor of their candidate. It is important to have clear terms of service related to comments and how a site will handle them. (For legal information, see "Terms of Use," 2008.)

- The sheer volume of comments can be challenging to monitor. There is no easy answer to shorten that time. Giving users the means to report objectionable content can help empower them and assist with monitoring.

- People making comments may not be who they say they are. Ultimately there is no way to determine without error who is on the other end of a conversation online. Even an IP address is no guarantee of personal identity. Ashby Jones, who has experience with the *Journal*'s Law Blog, pointed out this challenge. "You get people writing in who claim to be people that they're not, and you've got to go sniff those out and delete them. That's an imprecise art." Jones offered these thoughts on how he uncovers pretenders.

> It's more a feel thing than anything. But often, it's not hard to deduce that someone posting under the name "Samuel Alito" is not, in fact, the Supreme Court justice of the same name. The harder cases are those in which somebody pretends to be a lawyer involved in a case. Often, you'll just have to call to make sure it's that person and not an imposter.

With the increasing prominence of conversation as a dimension of online journalism, these challenges are likely to linger even though journalists may develop creative ways to manage them.

❖ VIRTUE AND CONVERSATION

As with discussion in previous chapters, the virtues necessary to strengthen the practice of journalism are implied rather than stated directly in the comments of the journalists interviewed and the way they do their work. But three virtues connect closely to the pursuit of standards of excellence in conversation: humility, honesty, and courage.

- The best bloggers are open to correction, clarification, or modification based on contributions from readers, as Boyle shows on his Cosmic Log blog. That kind of openness takes humility, unless one wants to be frustrated all the time reading comments from the audience. More generally, putting the public and conversation in a central place dethrones the journalist from the previous position of authority. Humility does not equate with abandoning editorial judgment, but if conversation is central, then public comments and the knowledge that they provide must be welcomed for whatever contributions they make.

- Honesty is also a key virtue because a journalist inviting and displaying reader comments has to be transparent about criticism and correction that may come with those contributions.

- Journalists who monitor discussion on controversial topics have to display courage to let difficult discussions proceed, as well as to step in when threads of conversation get out of hand. The careful balance discussed earlier between monitoring and allowing discussions to proceed robustly calls for exercise of courage with particular discernment. Courage is also necessary at the front end when it comes to initiating discussion on sensitive issues.

Individual journalists practicing these virtues strengthen the practice of journalism and help make possible the kinds of excellence this book has been examining.

❖ ON-THE-JOB PROFILE: ERIC ZORN
FACING THE DAILY CHALLENGES

Photo 6.2 Eric Zorn said doing the Change of Subject political blog for the *Chicago Tribune* takes a thick skin and a willingness to work long hours, along with an ability to keep the rest of life in balance.

Eric Zorn shows that a blogger's work is almost never done. Zorn, a veteran columnist for the *Chicago Tribune,* started the *Tribune's* first blog, Change of Subject, in 2003. He posts entries about everything from sports to music, but the focus is on Chicago and Illinois politics. The blog was Zorn's idea, so he has the freedom to carve out his responsibilities.

A walk through one day on the job— February 8, 2010—shows how much he has taken on.

Zorn said two stories were on people's minds around the area going into that Monday: the Super Bowl the day before and the resignation (during the game) of Democratic lieutenant governor candidate Scott Lee Cohen, who was caught up in scandal. During a Super Bowl party Sunday night, Zorn had already posted a blog entry asking people for their thoughts on the resignation.

Starting at 5 a.m. Monday, while he was sleeping, a digital recorder was recording the WGN morning show, a middle-of-the-road news talk program that often includes newsmaker interviews. Zorn got up about 6:30, traded out recorders, and started skimming past traffic and weather reports to hear what the talk was about—while helping his kids get ready for school.

As soon as they were out the door, he started reading newspapers to see what they were covering as he thought about what to write about later in the day for his Tuesday column in the *Tribune*. He also checked in online to see what local political blogs were saying.

> I find that the conversation, whether it's digital or broadcast, is just sort of stimulating to me. I see the arguments, I see people making points. I reflect on those points, I try to get a sense of where the argument is and where it might be going and what I have to say about it. . . . If you just look in the newspaper for what's news you may have missed something that happened overnight, or happened in the morning.

His first blog post of the morning, at 10:02, was about the 10-year anniversary of the death of a morning radio host in a plane crash. It was a big news event when it happened, but it got only two comments on the blog.

He put up another post on local transit cutbacks, again to see if people would react. Only eight commented.

Along with everything else, Zorn was checking a Facebook feed where he posts links to these items. He also looked through Twitter to see what people were saying about Super Bowl ads, and at 10:14 he posted links to some of them.

On he went, posting ideas about replacement running mates for the Democratic nominee for governor, Pat Quinn, knowing there was talk about that on other political blogs and the radio. He also went on the radio himself to do a phone interview about the same thing. Later, he would get the audio and have to edit it down before posting it.

At noon, he made the final call on what he would write about for his column—Cohen's resignation—and e-mailed his boss. From noon to 3 he focused on writing the column. But every 15 or 20 minutes, he would monitor the comments on his posts, which he used to approve before they went up on the site but now checks after the fact. "Now the conversation goes on," he said, "and I have to go through and go back and make sure no one's trying to sell T-shirts or use racial epithets, or swear words." Occasionally he jumps in and comments directly in a discussion thread as well. Sometimes that is to challenge someone who isn't bringing thoughtful opinion, but he said conversations with readers online often sharpen his own thinking.

Other posts followed as the day went on, including a comment from a reader that originated as an e-mail directly to him.

Even though he focuses on local issues, he also weighed in on a controversy over Sarah Palin's comments about the word "retard."

At dinnertime, his workday pauses but doesn't end. Right after dinner, he downloaded an interview with Cohen from another radio station, WLS, listened to it while he was walking the dog and returning a video, and then posted critical words about the interview. The post shows his blunt and colorful voice.

> This is cringeworthy. Don and Roma Wade slobbering all over Scott Lee Cohen this morning and lobbing total softballs at him attempting to feed his sense of victimhood and gin up discontent among Democrats—gee maybe they can coax him into running as an independent?
>
> A full hour in the studio and not one tough question. And not even a hint that they appreciate the irony that, suddenly, the plight of a disgraced Democrat has attracted the interest and concern of their right-wing listeners. I don't recall these sorts of expressions of outrage and dismay at WLS when Republican U.S. Senate primary winner Jack Ryan was "forced" to step aside. Did I just miss them? Or is this every bit the orgy of shamelessness it sounds like? (Zorn, 2010)

After a lighthearted post about a reading of *Mike Mulligan and His Steam Shovel*, just another part of keeping interest on the blog, he went to the *Tribune* website to retrieve his edited column. He cut and pasted the column, reformatted it for the blog, got a photo of Cohen from the *Tribune* photo gallery, and pasted it in. At 10:25 he put it on his blog. But he wasn't done. He read the column into a microphone to create an audio version and posted it.

And then he was done—about 11 p.m.—except that he went down to watch a recorded version of the 10 o'clock TV news to look ahead to the next day. The day was typical, and it was also filled with checks of e-mail and various distractions.

Zorn said it is a challenge "to keep up with all the input that comes in, to make sure that you're not missing things in the comments, make sure that you're not missing things in the e-mail, to make sure that you're not going over things too lightly." It's difficult to dig deeply into anything, he said, when he spends time "skimming the surface, talking to people for five minutes, reading shorter news stories, the whole kind of blip, blip, blip."

It takes a thick skin to do the job well, Zorn said. And "you cannot have a 9-to-5 mentality." It's crucial to be interested in the subject. But it's also important to keep a balance despite the constant flow of the work. "You have to sort of be willing to immerse yourself in that, and then you also have to be able to lift your head out of it periodically, because otherwise you'd just go nuts, alienate your family and friends."

❖ REFERENCES

Anderson, R., Dardenne, R., & Killenberg, G. M. (1994). *The conversation of journalism: Communication, community, and news.* Westport, CT: Praeger.

Black, J. (Ed.). (1997). *Mixed news: The public/civic/communitarian journalism debate.* Mahwah, NJ: Erlbaum.

Borden, S. L. (2007). *Journalism as practice: MacIntyre, virtue ethics and the press.* Burlington, VT: Ashgate.

Boyle, A. (2009, June 16). The universe in your head. *msnbc.com.* Retrieved February 16, 2010, from http://cosmiclog.msnbc.msn.com/archive/2009/06/16/1966953.aspx

Commission on Freedom of the Press. (1947). *A free and responsible press; A general report on mass communication: Newspapers, radio, motion pictures, magazines, and books.* Chicago: University of Chicago.

Faber, J. (2007, April 12). CBS fires Don Imus over racial slur. *CBS News.* Retrieved February 16, 2010, from http://www.cbsnews.com/stories/2007/04/12/national/main2675273.shtml

Groups. (n.d.). *washingtonpost.com.* Retrieved February 16, 2010, from http://www.washingtonpost.com/wp-dyn/content/discussions/groups/

Jones, A. (2009, March 11). Junk the LSAT? Making the case for a better test. *WSJ.com.* Retrieved February 16, 2010, from http://blogs.wsj.com/law/2009/03/11/junk-the-lsat-making-the-case-for-a-better-test/tab/article/

Kovach, B., & Rosenstiel, T. (2007). *The elements of journalism: What newspeople should know and the public should expect* (Rev. ed.). New York: Three Rivers Press.

Lambeth, E., & Craig, D. (1995). Civic journalism as research. *Newspaper Research Journal, 16*(2), 148–160. Retrieved from Communication & Mass Media Complete database.

Live coverage. (n.d.). *msnbc.com.* Retrieved February 14, 2010, from http://www.msnbc.msn.com/id/31768552

MacIntyre, A. (2007). *After virtue* (3rd ed.). Notre Dame, IN: University of Notre Dame Press.

Mill, J. S. (2003). *Utilitarianism and on liberty: Including Mill's 'Essay on Bentham' and selections from the writings of Jeremy Bentham and John Austin* (M. Warnock, Ed.). Oxford, England: Blackwell.

Milton, J. (2003). Aeropagitica. In M. Y. Hughes (Ed.), *John Milton: Complete poems and major prose* (pp. 716–749). Indianapolis, IN: Hackett. (Reprinted from *John Milton: Complete poems and major prose,* by M. Y. Hughes, Ed., 1957, New York: Prentice Hall; original work published 1644.)

The New York Times. (2010). *Facebook.* Retrieved February 16, 2010, from http://www.facebook.com/nytimes

Publishing the statements and content of others. (2009, August 25). *Citizen Media Law Project.* Retrieved February 16, 2010, from http://www.citmedia law.org/legal-guide/publishing-statements-and-content-others

Silverman, R. E. (2009, March 12). A parent's nightmare: Leaving your child in the car. *WSJ.com.* Retrieved February 16, 2010, from http://blogs.wsj.com/ juggle/2009/03/12/a-parents-nightmare-leaving-your-child-in-the-car/tab/article/

Society of Professional Journalists. (1996). Code of ethics. *Society of Professional Journalists.* Retrieved February 16, 2010, from http://www.spj.org/ethics code.asp

Terms of use. (2008, September 12). *Citizen Media Law Project.* Retrieved February 16, 2010, from http://www.citmedialaw.org/legal-guide/terms-use

Zorn, E. (2010, February 8). Using Scott Lee Cohen. *chicagotribune.com.* Retrieved May 20, 2010, from http://blogs.chicagotribune.com/news_ columnists_ezorn/2010/02/using-scott-lee-cohen.html

❖ COMPANION WEBSITE

Visit the companion website at **www.sagepub.com/craigstudy** for links to examples of online journalism.

7

Beyond the Big Guys

Independent and Community
Journalism Online

S o far, this book has focused on online journalism from the standpoint of large, mainstream news sites while also pointing to the
ways individual citizens are contributing to reporting and discussion. This chapter takes an important turn to look at what smaller
organizations and individuals—both people with professional journalism backgrounds and others—are doing online. Some of the most interesting news and conversation about issues is coming from outside the
big outlets, and the big ones are not always the fastest to innovate. So
it is important to step back and do a study in contrasts. With the rapid
change in user preferences and the uncertain economics of online news
in the early 21st century, the landscape of independent and community
journalism is shifting quickly. But these smaller sites are helping to
drive forward the development of journalism as a practice.

Table 7.1 draws a map of the landscape beyond the big guys. It
includes a range of shapes and sizes of online ventures such as

Table 7.1   The Landscape of Independent and Community Journalism

Organization/ activity	Place of citizen versus professional journalist in activity	Cooperative activity?	Has a public purpose?*
Smaller mainstream news organizations (connected with newspapers, TV, radio outlets)	Professional primary/citizen secondary	Yes	Yes
Online-based journalism ventures— community or specialty, profit or nonprofit	Professional usually primary, but citizens may play key role	Yes, including interaction with citizens	Yes, though may focus on particular issues
Citizen news sites	Citizen primary, but professional may play key role	Yes with interaction among citizens	Yes
Independent blogs	Varies depending on the blog	Yes, including interaction with citizens	Varies
Independent users of social media	Citizen primary	Yes but may be very informal	Varies

*Related to Borden's (2007) *telos* for journalism: "to help citizens know well in the public sphere."

community sites connected with smaller newspapers, new for-profit and not-for-profit journalism ventures, and citizen news sites and blogs—and beyond that, individuals using social media such as Facebook and Twitter. The purposes, organization, and backgrounds of these sites raise important questions about the boundaries of the practice of journalism.

This chapter will:

- Look at three sites—one tied to a smaller mainstream news organization and two independent startups with roots in professional journalism—through the eyes of a key individual who has worked at each. Following MacIntyre's (2007) framework again, the discussion will shed light on their perspectives about excellence and the challenges they face, as well as how they strive to overcome those challenges.

- Look beyond sites directly connected with professional journalism to the place of citizen journalism and social media in the development of journalism as a practice.

❖ PERSPECTIVES FROM THREE SMALLER ORGANIZATIONS

Excellence shows up in organizations of all sizes. The first of the three is much smaller than the big operations discussed in earlier chapters—but still far from the smallest end of the spectrum. The other two are about as small as they get but still manage to do journalism worthy of the best traditions of the field. Each stands clearly in these traditions but has tried to be innovative in the new-media environment and engage with citizens.

Roanoke.com

The site is connected with *The Roanoke Times,* a newspaper of about 90,000 circulation owned by Landmark Communications. The site serves communities in the mountains, hills, and valleys of western Virginia—particularly Roanoke, population about 95,000. Roanoke .com has been recognized for excellence by several awards, including the 2007 Online News Association award for breaking news on small sites for its coverage of the shootings on the Virginia Tech campus and other awards for overall quality ("Awards and Recognition," n.d.).

Seth Gitner, who was multimedia editor for Roanoke.com before becoming a professor at Syracuse University in fall 2009, played a key role in the online operation for several years. He worked with a small team of editors and producers creating online content including

Photo 7.1   Seth Gitner, former multimedia editor for Roanoke.com, played a key role in creating online content including special multimedia projects.

multimedia. He worked with audio, video, and interactive elements and built websites for special projects. He said the site's special projects focus on community news topics that connect with readers, such as a project on aging and one on a local art museum. (For links to multimedia projects the organization has done, see "Recent Multimedia," 2010.) Gitner won numerous awards for his work, underlining his desire to pursue excellence.

Some of the aspects of excellence discussed throughout this book surfaced in Gitner's comments about Roanoke.com in early 2009. The centrality of conversation showed up when he talked about special projects in newspapers versus online. A key focus of the work on a project after it initially goes up on the site is trying to spur conversation and giving people reason to return—not only right after the project goes online but also months later. That was a goal with "Age of Uncertainty" (Gitner et al., n.d.), which was about aging in Southwest Virginia. The project was set up online with a blog for reporter Beth Macy, Gitner says.

> She had a blog on it so that she could post: What are your ideas? What are you going through? Are you having the same experiences that this person is having with their husband? And there's opportunity there to build that conversation, to build that audience and get people to come back.

In addition, comment space with each story posted to this site gave people a chance to respond to the stories and for Macy to respond to them. The number of comments on the blog and the stories online turned out to be relatively small, but creating a conversation space was important for an issue with significant implications for the community. The site also provided comprehensive treatment of the topic through multiple elements including photo galleries, videos, interactive assessment tools, and a searchable database of senior care facilities. These features enhanced both the storytelling and the ability of the audience to learn about the topic.

When the shootings occurred at Virginia Tech, Gitner landed in the middle of one of the biggest breaking stories of the decade. He got to Blacksburg quickly from Roanoke the first day. He covered press conferences but put most of his energy into doing stories that were not at the core of the breaking events—but stories that were important because they showed how people were responding and dealing with this tragedy. He worked with a reporter, Evelio Contreras, who later became a multimedia producer.

> He and I basically went out and covered stories that were how people were coping with it, what they were doing—giving hugs around town, people doing hand painting, things on the drill field—that type of story, rather than the latest thing. (For examples, see Contreras & Gitner, 2007a and 2007b.)

These human elements would have connected deeply with his audience in the communities of this region. He covered this story in a way that made the most of the limited number of personnel in a smaller organization. His content could not be as comprehensive as it might have been for a larger organization, but he tried to choose the storytelling focus carefully within the limitations he faced.

Screenshot 7.1 After the Virginia Tech shootings, Seth Gitner and reporter Evelio Contreras focused on stories that showed how people were responding and dealing with the tragedy.

Like the big sites discussed in this book, Roanoke.com has pursued standards of excellence in the best of its online journalism. In the perspective of MacIntyre's (2007) framework, this work can help achieve goods internal to the practice of journalism. For example, pursuing comprehensive coverage of an important topic such as aging can help advance knowledge of community needs, personal challenges, and available resources. The good of newness is advanced through coverage of breaking news that goes beyond basic facts and circumstances—and in the case of the Virginia Tech coverage, knowledge of a tragedy deeply important to the area grows deeper with portrayals of the human impact.

The challenges to excellence look similar in some ways to those of larger organizations, but some of these limitations are more evident. Time and staffing constraints are inevitable in all news operations, even the largest, but they can hit home more sharply in a smaller organization. Gitner praised *Roanoke Times* Editor Carole Tarrant for her willingness to allow time for him to develop a strong online story idea. But he noted that larger organizations might have more people with the right skill sets or more resources to acquire the skills, enabling them to do a project faster.

It may be inevitable that the standard of comprehensiveness in content is sacrificed more frequently in smaller organizations—although it is evident that Roanoke.com has put depth of resources into selected multimedia projects. And it is difficult to do regular multimedia coverage of breaking stories. Gitner said doing multimedia on breaking news "depends on the size of the event." The event "has to be something substantial for us to move our resources around and cancel things that are happening in our small team to make it."

In a profit-making institution such as *The Roanoke Times,* it is inevitable that the external good of profit will constrain excellence. However, it was evident from Gitner that the organization has committed substantial resources to the pursuit of excellence in online work. Virtues, a key part of MacIntyre's (2007) framework, seem to play a role in the level of quality in the organization. Gitner showed the virtue of initiative to learn skills or find others with skills necessary to pursue multimedia projects. And he noted that Tarrant "allows for creativity to exist," allowing time for him to work to develop strong multimedia pieces. Gitner made the most of the opportunity for creativity while working with a small staff. The initiative and creativity, combined with the support from management, have made strong work possible within the constraints of the institution.

QuincyNews.org

QuincyNews.org is far smaller in staff and reach than Roanoke.com, but it has reflected standards of excellence in its own way. The site serves Quincy, Illinois, a Mississippi River town of 40,000. Bob Gough, a former broadcast and newspaper journalist, founded the site in April 2008. As of early 2009, he was the only staff member and sold ads as well as reporting the news, but by later in the year he had hired a sales representative on commission.

The site includes news articles he writes, his blog, including live reports from city meetings, comments from readers, "vox populi" items contributed from organizations in the community, and links to regional news items from other organizations. Gough regards the site's most distinctive contribution as watchdog coverage of government, something he sees as lacking from other local media outlets. He developed a news-sharing partnership with a local AM radio station. Gough watched traffic on the site grow from about 500 visits a day to about 1,400 after a flood in June 2008, and the numbers then went down but rose to average 2,700 a day by November 2009. Those may sound like small numbers, but the site had attracted more than 75 different businesses as advertisers and satisfied

Photo 7.2   Bob Gough, who started QuincyNews.org both reporting news and selling ads, covers city government aggressively in Quincy, Illinois.

two investors who helped get the project off the ground. Gough was making enough to keep the site afloat.

Like Gitner, Gough looks at excellence in ways that line up with the standards discussed in the rest of this book. But again, things look different in some details. Gough sees the watchdog function as the core of excellence in online journalism but "virtually nonexistent" in traditional media.

The financial troubles that big media's having really make it tough for them to go do the kind of watchdog, good government journalism that is needed in this country now more than ever because of all the media cutbacks across the board. Investigative units are suffering, smaller newsrooms, there's just fewer journalists out there at the old big media. So I think starting what we've started here,

QuincyNews.org, is pretty important and I think it's the future because somebody's gotta watch 'em. I mean, government, especially here in the great state of Illinois, time and time again proves that if you don't watch them, they will do things that are unethical, and the politicians will do things to line their own pockets. And it is as important a time as ever for a free press, but the free press in and of itself is very diluted. And that really bothers me.

Borden (2007) placed reporting at the center of the tradition of the practice of journalism, and Gough's comments reflect a concern for a key piece of the work of reporting. Vigorous pursuit of watchdog journalism should be part of the comprehensiveness of both online and old-line journalism. Gough has carried out his mission by reporting aggressively on city government, including a story showing that the city's information technology director had a criminal record, having been convicted of theft for manipulating computer data in a previous job (Gough, 2008). Gough's coverage of the story and following developments included a link to a police report (2008) and a document with grand jury testimony (B. Gough, 2009). Those links reflect the idea of comprehensiveness online discussed in Chapter 4 because this original documentation provides background source material that readers can look at for themselves as they evaluate the story.

Gough's blog provides a different twist on the standard of speed and accuracy with depth in breaking news. He routinely sits down with his computer at meetings in the city and blogs live, typing from the start of the meeting or before to the finish. For example, he blogged on March 30, 2009, from a Quincy mayoral forum. He opened the post this way:

> We're blogging live from the YP Quincy Mayoral Forum. Should start shortly. Event is being held in the Lindsay Room at the Oakley-Lindsay Center. Sounds like about 30 people attend. Good number for a weekday. (J. R. Gough, 2009)

He freely acknowledges in the post that he is not typing word for word, but he goes on to render both questions and answers in the forum in as much detail as he can. He sees this approach as giving readers a clear and straightforward picture of what's happening:

> Maybe it gives them a little more sense of being there because I don't do a lot of editing. I just kind of type as fast as I can and listen to what the people have to say and put it down. And I don't have time to put an opinion in that. That's raw, that's straight, that's the reporter's notebook right there.

Gough said he wants community involvement and wants people to form opinions and comment on the blog, and he sees the blog as providing something more interactive than a story. Even as he was writing the blog that day, he was getting comments by e-mail (though he did not have time to approve them to put up).

Gough's live blog meets the standard of speed and gets readers more material than they would receive from a story in traditional journalistic format. In one sense, he does not meet the standard for the accuracy part since he may not capture everything word for word, but the detail he provides and the reflection of the actual flow of discussion may give readers a more accurate picture of what is happening than a traditional story.

His interaction with the community on the blog—through his direct and informal writing as well as reader comments—also makes conversation a central element. He prizes that kind of interaction and sees it as lacking in old media.

> I want people to have strong opinions. I want them to be for me or against me, but I want them to have an opinion, I want them to have an impact in their community. And I think that's one thing that is certainly needed, is the give and take. I want to fact-check the government, I want to fact-check myself. I mean this morning I had a typo in a story, I had somebody kick me an e-mail, "Hey, you left a letter out in your word."

Gough's interest in give and take, and his openness to correction on the site, are both part of making conversation central. He also leaves the door open for open-ended story development if readers point him to new facts or angles to pursue.

Without idealizing Gough's work, it can be said that he is pursuing in some ways the standards of journalistic excellence examined throughout this book, or providing the environment in which he or others can pursue them in the future. He is also helping to meet the internal goods of the practice of journalism. Knowledge and inquiry about issues important in the community are advanced through coverage of city government through traditional stories and blogging, coupled with the opportunity for readers to respond and discuss issues and the availability of original source material. The site meets the good of newness in a distinctive way through his live blogging of meetings.

The engagement with the community, particularly because it involves local governance, advances the good of fostering community by connecting people around important topics. Even if the number of people connected is not huge, it is a step forward for them. Thus, like the best larger sites, QuincyNews.org bolsters and alters previous ideas about what excellence in journalism means.

As for challenges, the fact that Gough is the only news staff member creates an acute challenge to his ability to edit and, more broadly, to do as many stories as he might like. It is impossible for any news organization to cover all government bodies all the time in great depth, but Gough feels the pain of limitations more greatly than journalists even in small mainstream outlets. He may have rough edges in stories that his readers are left to correct since he cannot, and other stories may simply go undone.

Another challenge Gough faced for a time was the fact that he had to both cover news and sell advertising—two functions that have traditionally been separated in journalism and can create conflicts of interest if they are together. And if he does inject opinion into any of his writing, that sits in tension with the tradition of separation between opinion and news coverage.

The place of external goods, though, in these challenges looks different from what it does in larger, established institutions such as NYTimes.com or even Roanoke.com. Profit shows up in his operation as much as a vehicle for improvement and expanded coverage as it does a temptation to depart from good journalism. If Gough made more money, he could hire more people and cover more stories. The pressure to make money to expand did squeeze together advertising and news functions because Gough had to keep working both sides on his own—at least until hiring a sales representative, though not full time. Overall, though, it appears that Gough is—at least in the short term—bucking the trend of cutbacks in journalism because of financial pressures and paying for local, watchdog journalism. The fact that he is pulling this off even for a while suggests the virtues of perseverance and initiative on his part.

West Seattle Blog

West Seattle Blog (online at westseattleblog.com) is another news operation trying to make enough money through advertising to do good journalism—though its broad use of citizen reporting gives it a lot in common with not-for-profit citizen journalism sites. Started in 2005, it is operated by the husband–wife team of Tracy Record, copublisher/ editor, and Patrick Sand, copublisher/business development director. The site covers West Seattle, an area of about 58,000 southwest of downtown bordering on Puget Sound. It is a blog in format but, unlike many blogs, includes much original reporting—along with comments and contributions from members of the community. Like Gough, Record is a former broadcast news person well aware of the traditions of journalism. She resigned as assistant news director at a Seattle TV station in December 2007 to work on the blog full time. Her previous work included being executive producer of abcnews.com and other roles at TV stations, newspapers, and radio stations. It also included three Emmy awards (About, n.d.).

Record's perspective on the work of their site, which she discussed in e-mails in March and October 2009, reflects the standards of excellence in this book. She thinks about the site from the standpoint of a broadcaster:

> Our distinctive contribution is providing news, information, and discussion opportunities as the news happens, 24/7. My co-publisher husband and I both have broadcasting backgrounds and we see the site in more of an always-on two-way broadcasting mode, rather than as any sort of a "we publish, you react" static entity. The discussion is no small part of the coverage—when a breaking story is happening, whether it's a crime investigation or a weather emergency like our December 2006 windstorm or our December 2008 snowstorms, the information provided by community members adding comments, forum posts, e-mails, photos is a major part of the coverage, and such "crowdsourcing" is something that our primary competitor publicly dismissed and disregarded in the form of a published editorial, so it's clear that our site is the only place that will be "allowed" to happen.

This comment implies a view of journalism that closely connects to all four of the standards of excellence discussed earlier: speed and accuracy with depth, comprehensiveness, open-endedness in story development, and the centrality of conversation. While journalists with print backgrounds might think of online journalism in terms of a wire service, Record places the "always-on" aspect of the site in terms of broadcasting, another medium of high speed. But part of the speed of reporting comes through the work of community members whose responses enhance coverage as well as providing conversation about the topic. "Crowdsourcing" provides an element of comprehensiveness, particularly as citizens respond in numerous formats.

Record elaborated at length on how the public extends the site's ability to report in a variety of situations, large and small.

We can only find out so much by ourselves, no matter how many rocks we look under, public records we comb, streets we drive, calls we make.

Community members are thousands of eyes and ears—and with so much of what they contribute, whether as a "tip" or as a fullblown photo/text contribution, that means they get to tell thousands of their neighbors. We have examples large and small:

Small—a photo of a bird, taken by someone who had no idea what kind of bird; we didn't either, we published the photo and said so, and within an hour a dozen people had all identified it, helping not only the curious photographer but also educating hundreds/ thousands of others.

Bigger—every time a police helicopter spends more than a few minutes over a local neighborhood, people send us notes "what's going on"—even if we can't get official information immediately, we open a post about it, and while we pursue that official information, invariably "readers" who are close to whatever action is happening on the ground also find the post and leave comments telling what they are seeing, what they are hearing, even what they have been told by police officers who are on their street because of whatever the incident is. This in turn means that hundreds/thousands of other people can either take steps to protect themselves OR can rest easier knowing that the helicopter is actually dealing with something miles away.

Biggest—When we had that huge snow situation in December 2008, we had massive failures of public transportation, snow removal, trash pickup, and information systems related to some of those services. Comment threads on our ongoing snow coverage turned into sharing of very specific information: A certain bus finally showed up at a certain place at a certain time. Or, neighborhood X finally spotted a trash truck, three days late. Or, a snowplow was seen on street X, which hadn't been cleared in days. Etc. That information all enabled people to know when it was safe to go out, whether they needed to plot an alternate route to work, whether they should take their trash to the corner. None of this information was coming from the official sources due to various problems. So with our site as a platform, citizens managed to help each other.

Record's respect for contributions of readers is evident. Information from them has helped not only to satisfy curiosity, as with a bird species, but also to help others overcome system failure in major city services. These instances reflect excellence through the fostering of open-ended story development and conversation, as well as quicker and more comprehensive coverage than they alone could have provided.

Screenshot 7.2   Tracy Record's blog has done watchdog coverage important to West Seattle, including a story about waterproofing work at two city reservoirs that had to be redone thanks to leaks in the membranes used to cover the reservoirs.

As with the other sites discussed, it is not hard to see how pursuing these standards of excellence helps lead to the achievement of internal goods such as knowledge, inquiry, newness, and fostering community. Record's own reporting has included watchdog coverage, such as a story about waterproofing work being redone at two city reservoirs thanks to hundreds of leaks in the membranes used to cover the reservoirs (Record, 2009). This kind of work, combined with substantial citizen contributions, enhances knowledge and inquiry, as well as advancing the good of newness. The opportunity for conversation and mutual pursuit of answers to questions as events develop in the community has the potential to foster community among citizens in West Seattle. Again it is important not to idealize the work of the site because no journalist can meet standards of excellence perfectly. But a site like this, run by someone with strong grounding in high-quality journalism and openness to making the most of the insights of citizens, can help to reshape understanding of what excellence in journalism looks like. That new understanding can come through demonstration of the power of online conversation to engage citizens in a community more fully, along with the ability of trained journalists to pursue the craft aggressively themselves while also drawing substantially from the wisdom of community members.

Again, time constraints thanks to staffing limitations are at the core of the challenges for this operation. For Record, these constraints hit home in their impact on thoroughness.

> Our primary challenge is in thoroughness. Not thoroughness necessarily for an individual story, but for covering everything we want to cover—while we publish an average of a dozen items a day, there are probably two dozen stories a day I would like to tell, and even with the help of paid freelancers and unofficial community contributors, time just runs out. One of our primary hopes for increasing revenue is the ability to hire more people, so that we can tell those TWO dozen stories each day—and hopefully even more.

Comprehensiveness in the broad sense, then, suffers thanks to the combination of limited staffing with limited revenue and the time crunch that creates. So again, as in the case with the Quincy site, another fledgling institution, profit appears not so much as an external good that endangers journalism as a necessary means to enhance it.

Overcoming the limitations on staffing and time to be thorough in this setting takes creative effort. Record recounted a situation in which the site provided exclusive coverage of a murder case from beginning to end. (See the accompanying box for an ethical dilemma she encountered in her coverage.)

NAMING (AND UNNAMING?) IN ONLINE CRIMINAL COVERAGE

Tracy Record, editor of the West Seattle Blog, has a lot of journalism experience to fall back on in her role as the single professional editor on her community site, including a decade as one of the top managers in newsrooms. But that doesn't make every decision easy.

One challenging ethical dilemma came with the coverage of a fatal shooting inside a car near a beach neighborhood:

It seemed at the start like a cut-and-dried murder case. The teenage suspect surrendered within two days. He was charged as an adult and we published his name. Then—a twist: His defense turned out to be the contention that he had been sexually abused since childhood by the man he shot dead in the car that day, who allegedly had stalked him across multiple states to continue the "relationship." [See "59th/Admiral Shooting Suspect's Defense Argument," 2007.] When this was officially filed in court, I decided that as there was a chance he really had been a long-term victim of sexual abuse, I would stop publishing his name. However, I did not go back and delete it from past stories, and to this day it's still out there in the archives. I do not believe in deleting published content unless something hugely dramatic necessitates it—I feel to some degree it would be like expecting a newspaper to "unpublish" something—it's out there, it's been out there.

Record's ethical challenge included a dimension particularly significant in online journalism. She had to decide not only whether to name a suspect initially but also, given the unusually sensitive nature of the case, whether to allow the name to live on in online archives.

West Seattle Blog was the only news organization that kept following this case, Record said. Finally, at the end of the trial, the defendant was found not guilty by reason of self-defense.

I knew I had made the right decision. But I really just made it up on the fly. I would have lobbied to do the same thing if I had still been in my old-media job, but I might not have won the fight if my boss had disagreed. I also wonder sometimes what would have happened if another media organization had decided to cover the trial and decided to keep using the young man's name, while we did not—how would our readers have reacted?

Record faces many decisions daily as she juggles responsibilities. How to handle the naming was a quick decision but an important one.

What ethical values were at issue? From the standpoint of duty-based ethics, seeking truth and minimizing harm are key principles. Seeking and reporting truth, as the Society of Professional Journalists ethics code (1996) calls for, suggests the suspect should be named because the name is public information—and, as a practical matter,

(Continued)

(Continued)

particularly public once the trial begins. The idea of full reporting also supports keeping the name in the stories in the database. On the other hand, though, the principle of minimizing harm calls into question whether this young man should be named—at least once it has come to light that he may have been a victim of child sexual abuse and stalking by the man who was killed. Taking into account both principles supports both dimensions of Record's decision:

- The normal public disclosure of a suspect's name along with the recognition that the online archive is a record of information already made public.

- The extra sensitivity to the defendant when the circumstances came to light.

From the standpoint of virtue-based ethics, the decision she made suggests an exercise of a proper measure of compassion—following Aristotle's mean, which calls for striving for a balance between vices of deficiency and excess. Deficiency in relation to compassion would have meant continuing to name the young man without consideration of the impact on him. Excess would have meant considering only that and removing his name from earlier stories. The decision Record made— even though she was not pondering Aristotle at the time—represents an appropriate mean between these extremes.[1]

She followed the case, involving a man shot dead only a few blocks from a beach neighborhood popular throughout the city, until it went to trial.

> My challenge here was that I could not do the job of running a full-service news site AND do justice to gavel-to-gavel trial coverage. My husband needed to focus on running the business side of the site, and his newsgathering strengths don't really include the type of work that I would have been neglecting by sitting in a courtroom all day for several weeks, so he couldn't really take on the editor role if I removed myself by focusing on the trial. But I had a feeling no one else would bother to cover this trial, so I needed to find a way that we could. I found

---

[1]For more reading on application of the mean to journalism, see Patterson & Wilkins (2008).

a freelance reporter who had contacted me recently looking for work, and who happened to be able to commit to covering the entire trial—with an agreement that if she had a conflict one day or another, she would let me know in advance, and I could go to court that day. She filed reports each day, and then when the jury started deliberating, I told her I was hoping to also be in the courtroom for the verdict-reading, so I could publish it immediately to our site—I made arrangements to be in the area during deliberations, and when she called me, it only took me a 20-minute uphill walk to get there.

Record and the freelancer stayed to wrap up the coverage after the verdict, and the site continued following later developments in the case. With her staffing limitations, Record had to exercise ingenuity and perseverance to see the coverage through to the end. Beyond these virtues that are implied in the handling of this coverage (and compassion in the handling of naming, as the accompanying box shows), her attitude toward reader contributions and their central role in enhancing the site's journalism implies a humility toward her own work and its relationship to what citizens provide.

The Smaller Organizations in Perspective

Taken together, the work of individuals at these three smaller operations highlights the fact that journalists without the staffs of big media outlets can report quickly and correctly—and powerfully, as Gitner did from Virginia Tech. But they may need to leave more stories undone in order to do well the ones they choose to cover. As Gough shows with his inclusion of links to public documents, even a one-man show can approach a standard of comprehensiveness in a story simply by providing these civic raw materials for citizens to examine. Record's openness to citizens' insights on all kinds of topics shows how the combination of experience in the traditions of journalism and respect for the promise of public knowledge can help make the most of the open-ended possibilities of online story development and empower conversation.

The challenges created by limited staffing are evident in a relatively small operation like Roanoke.com but painfully obvious in the Quincy and West Seattle operations. It takes a particular degree of perseverance to create excellent work against that backdrop. The place of the external good of profit, though, looks considerably different from the way it does at big news outlets. Large media companies are vulnerable to cutbacks to maintain past expectations of high profits. By contrast, an operation run by one or two people is vulnerable to collapse without enough profit. It is more obvious how profit can help to fuel good journalism when the additional profit may double the staff.

It is encouraging that strong reporting shows up at the core of the values of the journalists at the two smallest sites. Journalists working with both nonprofit and for-profit business models recognize that watchdog journalism monitoring governments and other institutions is vulnerable in the climate of financial and organizational upheaval in the news media in the early 21st century. The passion that both Gough and Record show for reporting re-centers the discussion of standards of excellence on the good that journalism can do for citizens. Borden's (2007) *telos* for journalism of knowing well in the public sphere stands a much better chance of being met when the content at the core of quick, accurate, comprehensive coverage online includes attention to the health of the institutions in that public sphere. As community and independent online journalists pursue standards of excellence with this coverage at the core, they have at least as important a role to play in reshaping understanding of journalistic excellence as their counter-parts in big media.

❖ CITIZEN JOURNALISM, SOCIAL MEDIA, AND JOURNALISM AS A PRACTICE

Beyond the world of online journalism occupied by people paid as pro-fessional journalists lies the very large world of various groups of citi-zens, independent bloggers, and people simply posting information through social media such as Twitter and Facebook. This world is highly diverse in size of operation, degree of specialization in focus, and purpose. Many occupants of this world would call themselves journal-ists; many others would not. Their activity tiptoes around the bound-aries of journalism as a practice, but it has huge implications for the development of the practice and its impact. This chapter will close by looking at some of those implications using the three issues shown in Table 7.1 earlier in this chapter: the role of professional journalists ver-sus citizens, the cooperative dimension of the work, and its purpose.

The Role of Professional Journalists Versus Citizens

Journalists have a special ethical responsibility, from MacIntyre's (2007) perspective, as bearers of the tradition of journalism and part of its moral community. But the work of citizens is also important to the health of journalism as a practice because of what they can contribute to the pursuit of knowledge and community. It is important, additionally, because citizens themselves may seek to adopt the best standards of journalism in their work.

The Knight Citizen News Network's database includes nearly 800 citizen media sites in North America (Directory of Citizen Media Sites, n.d). Some of these sites involve professional journalists along with citizens who are not formally journalists, while others do not. Bloggers, a group that overlaps with citizen journalists, also include many people with backgrounds in journalism. Technorati's "State of the Blogosphere 2009" stated that 35% of bloggers surveyed "have worked within the traditional media as a writer, reporter, producer, or on-air personality" (Sussman, 2009).

But whether or not professional journalists are involved, citizens doing solidly developed reporting greatly expand the ability of a community to learn about itself and inquire more deeply about public issues. Some of these sites have received funding from organizations such as the John S. and James L. Knight Foundation. J-Lab: The Institute for Interactive Journalism has helped to fund a number of startup operations to do community news through the New Voices program (New Voices, n.d.) funded by the foundation. For example, one 2010 grant is supporting development of a site to provide news about challenging issues in Maine's fishing communities. Another is to support starting a news site in San Jose, California, aimed at covering issues that affect neighborhoods. Citizen journalism sites are vulnerable to falling into disuse for lack of time and funding, but the very fact that hundreds have sprung up across North America has provided a greatly broadened opportunity for civic learning and building of community connections.

The millions of blogs in existence are a more mixed group. Some cover issues with important public implications, while others focus on more personal concerns. Technorati's directory of blogs includes thousands about business and politics, but "living" topics account for the largest number. The blogs on living include religion and health but also topics with less public connection such as food, home, and travel ("Browse the Directory," n.d.). When bloggers do report with care on issues that affect the public in important ways, they advance the same cause as thoughtful professional journalists—and sometimes challenge them to do better work themselves. This accountability function alone should serve to foster excellence in the practice.

For sites where professionals and citizens work together, professionals can help pass on the standards of the practice through the way they discuss and critique stories. Beyond that, the widespread availability of training and resources for citizens on how to do journalism provides opportunities to learn and follow these standards. For example, the Knight Citizen News Network's site (Knight Citizen News Network, n.d.) has included learning modules on a number of topics such as interviewing and open government, along with links to advice resources and journalism training sites.

Another focus for communication of journalistic standards is sometimes citizen sites themselves. The Rapidian (therapidian.org), a citizen journalism site launched in 2009 in Grand Rapids, Michigan, provides a history of citizen journalism and its importance and offers tips and resources. The tips address a variety of issues including third-person writing, use of multiple sources, fact checking, and ethics ("Citizen Journalism 101," n.d.). Though these tips are not all original to them (Hall, n.d.), their use signals a priority on following important conventions of journalism. The organization's statement of values conveys the importance of inclusiveness, civility, and ethical reporting. The section about ethical reporting says:

Standards for Rapidian reporters include:

- Seek truth

- Be honest and fair

- Minimize harm

- Do not misrepresent

- Seek alternate sources and points of view

- Do not use reporting for personal gain. ("The Rapidian Statement of Values," n.d.)

Clearly, this organization decided it was a priority to follow high standards of journalism. Laying out standards does not, in itself, make contributors to a site journalists. But efforts like this help connect the formal practice of journalism to its close relatives.

The Role of Cooperative Activity

MacIntyre (2007) said practices are by nature cooperative, and Borden argued that this means individual publishing such as blogging does not fall under the category of journalism even though it is interactive in character (Borden, 2007, p. 26). But this is another place where the edges of the practice are likely to grow more fuzzy.

"Crowdsourcing,"[2] which Tracy Record uses in West Seattle, may look the same on citizens' sites and the blogs of nonjournalists who draw on the knowledge of their audiences—whether those are members of a geographical community or a community of interest. Beyond reporting, editing is often partially the province of the group, whether it is direct or by feedback. Robust individual sites often rely so heavily on interaction with others that the activity is essentially cooperative. Ever since sites such as Wikipedia popularized the idea that editing information should be a public process, the cooperative dimension of reporting done by individuals has taken on increasing importance. Still, though, cooperative activity alone does not make a site journalistic. High standards of fact checking are central to the traditions of the practice.

With the development of social media sites such as Facebook and Twitter, individuals gained the power to interact quickly and easily on small and large matters. Clearly much of this activity is focused on the personal lives of individuals and their opinions, apart from information of public significance. But as previous chapters have shown, these sites enable powerful communication about developing news events— such as the jet landing in the Hudson River or the service for Michael Jackson. Even though the individuals using these sites do not become journalists just by using them, they provide a level of communication such that they greatly enhance the cooperative nature of communication with both professional journalists and citizen reporters.

The Purpose of the Site

At the background of everything that goes on in the practice of journalism is its purpose, or *telos*, which Borden (2007) said "is to help citizens know well in the public sphere" (p. 50). It is not something journalists contemplate every day, but it occupies a central place in consideration of the practice. Looking at sites with this in mind highlights the huge range of intent behind communication of information online. Small or large sites that clearly identify themselves as doing journalism are likely to hold such a goal whether it is explicitly stated or well achieved. Citizen sites and individuals using social media might be passionately interested in contributing to people's understanding of issues, or might be focused on self-satisfaction or ill-founded opinion.

---

[2]For an article and resources on crowdsourcing, see Caplan (2010).

A high school student posting to a close friend on Facebook is probably not trying "to help citizens know well" (though a high school journalist might be). Neither is a blogger who uses his online platform to attack political opponents without regard to fairness or evidence. But helping citizens to know well can take in a huge range of topics—from the traditional hard-news beats of journalism to specialized information of science and business—and also a huge range of people. An individual tracking developments in a city planning commission and communicating about them on Twitter might help citizens in her community to know well concerning development issues. A blogger interviewing experts about policies on healthcare might also advance public knowledge.

One powerful example of a citizen helping other citizens know well is Jacqueline Dupree, whose site JDLand.com documents in detail the changes taking place because of development in the neighborhood where she lives in southeast Washington, D.C. She won a Knight-Batten citizen media award in 2008. The awards site described her effort as

> [a] one-woman citizen media project to document and inform a local community about real estate development issues. Armed with a digital camera, web production skills, mapping, and a mission to inform neighbors about construction projects, plans, meetings and its impact on daily life. ("2008 Winners," n.d.)

Among the tools she has added are Twitter and Facebook. She shows how one person not formally trained or employed as a journalist can do aggressive reporting harnessing multimedia tools and social media.

Citizen initiatives on topics important to large and small communities help fulfill the *telos* of journalism. They may not possess the staying power of traditional journalism because of a lack of organization, funding, or interest. But conscientious writers on citizen sites and blogs—and even on Twitter—potentially fill gaps that the relatively small number of professional journalists cannot. There is a danger that the *telos* of the practice will be fulfilled unevenly in different communities depending on the degree of citizen initiative. But this initiative may prove critical to the health of communities given the lack of a long-term business model to sustain commercial online journalism. The harsh backdrop of economics makes the role of citizen media even more important than before. Citizens who care deeply about life in their communities may help to preserve a sense of the *telos* of journalism while some professional journalists lose their jobs or their ability to do excellent work.

❖ REFERENCES

59th/Admiral shooting suspect's defense argument. (2007, October 29). *West Seattle Blog*. Retrieved February 21, 2010, from http://westseattleblog.com/2007/10/59thadmiral-shooting-suspects-defense-argument

2008 Winners. (2008). *J-Lab: The Institute for Interactive Journalism*. Retrieved February 21, 2010, from http://www.j-lab.org/awards/category/2008_winners/

About. (n.d.). *West Seattle Blog*. Retrieved February 16, 2010, from http://westseattleblog.com/wsb-faq

Awards and Recognition. (n.d.). *Roanoke.com*. Retrieved February 16, 2010, from http://www.roanoke.com/awards/

Borden, S. L. (2007). *Journalism as practice: MacIntyre, virtue ethics and the press.* Burlington, VT: Ashgate.

Browse the directory. (n.d.). *Technorati*. Retrieved May 26, 2010, from http://technorati.com/blogs/directory/

Caplan, J. (2010, May 12). 5 ways to crowdsource easily, legally & with quality. *Poynter Online*. Retrieved May 26, 2010, from http://www.poynter.org/column.asp?id=101&aid=183005

Citizen Journalism 101: Tips for producing a good story. (n.d.). *The Rapidian*. Retrieved February 16, 2010, from http://therapidian.org/tips

Contreras, E., & Gitner, S. (2007a, April 19). Video: Offering hugs in Blacksburg. *Roanoke.com*. Retrieved February 21, 2010, from http://www.roanoke.com/multimedia/video/wb/113867

Contreras, E., & Gitner, S. (2007b, April 19). Video: 'These are innocent handprints.' *Roanoke.com*. Retrieved February 21, 2010, from http://www.roanoke.com/multimedia/video/wb/113868

Directory of Citizen Media Sites. (n.d.). *Knight Citizen News Network.* Retrieved February 16, 2010, from http://www.kcnn.org/citmedia_sites/

Gitner, S., Boyer, T., Rooney, A., Martin, M., Chittum, M., & Jedlinsky, G. (n.d.). Age of uncertainty. *Roanoke.com*. Retrieved February 21, 2010, from http://blogs.roanoke.com/ageofuncertainty/

Gough, B. (2008, November 22). Man in charge of city computers has past theft conviction. *QuincyNews.org*. Retrieved February 21, 2010, from http://www.quincynews.org/local-news-archive/murphy-history-computer-story.html

Gough, B. (2009, March 31). Spring elaborates on IT, travel during WTAD interview. *QuincyNews.org*. Retrieved February 21, 2010, from http://www.quincynews.org/local-news-archive/spring-elaborates-on-it-airport-during-wtad-interview.html

Gough, J. R. (2009, March 30). YP Quincy mayoral forum blog transcript. *QuincyNews.org*. Retrieved February 21, 2010, from http://www.quincynews.org/blogs/jenkins-royko-grantland/yp-quincy-mayoral-forum-live-blog.html

Hall, J. (n.d.). *Beginning reporting: A web site for beginning reporters, those studying the craft and their teachers.* Retrieved February 16, 2010, from http://www.courses.vcu.edu/ENG-jeh/BeginningReporting/

Knight Citizen News Network. (n.d.). Retrieved February 21, 2010, from http://www.kcnn.org/site/

MacIntyre, A. (2007). *After virtue* (3rd ed.). Notre Dame, IN: University of Notre Dame Press.

New Voices. (n.d.). Retrieved February 21, 2010, from http://www.j-newvoices.org/

Patterson, P., & Wilkins, L. (2008). *Media ethics: Issues and cases* (6th ed.). New York: McGraw-Hill.

The Rapidian statement of values. (n.d.). *The Rapidian.* Retrieved February 21, 2010, from http://therapidian.org/values-statement

Recent multimedia. (2010). *Roanoke.com.* Retrieved May 26, 2010, from http://www.roanoke.com/clicks/default.aspx?url=/multimedia/video/wb/125747

Record, T. (2009, July 13). WSB exclusive: Hundreds of waterproofing leaks found at Myrtle, Beacon Reservoirs; "membranes" now being dug up and redone. *West Seattle Blog.* Retrieved February 21, 2010, from http://westseattleblog.com/2009/07/wsb-exclusive-hundreds-of-waterproofing-leaks-found-at-myrtle-beacon-reservoirs-membranes-now-being-dug-up-and-redone

Society of Professional Journalists. (1996). Code of ethics. *Society of Professional Journalists.* Retrieved February 16, 2010, from http://www.spj.org/ethicscode.asp

Sussman, M. (2009, October 19). Day 1: Who are the bloggers? SOTB 2009. *Technorati.* Retrieved February 16, 2010, from http://technorati.com/blogging/article/day-1-who-are-the-bloggers1

❖ COMPANION WEBSITE

Visit the companion website at **www.sagepub.com/craigstudy** for links to examples of online journalism.

8

The Future of Excellence in Online Journalism

Living in the World of Both-And

The preceding chapters have traveled a road through recent developments in online journalism. They have looked at the views and work of some talented and motivated people, mostly at large news organizations but also some small ones. Their thoughts have pointed to four developing standards of excellence in online journalism: speed and accuracy with depth in breaking news, comprehensiveness in content, open-endedness in story development, and the centrality of conversation. Philosopher Alasdair MacIntyre's theory of a practice (2007), along with the work of journalism ethicists Sandra Borden (2007) and Edmund Lambeth (1992), has helped to provide added insight about what these standards mean for the evolution of journalism and about the challenges that stand in the way. Table 8.1 shows the four standards of excellence and related issues from MacIntyre's theory: internal goods whose achievement helps reshape understanding of excellence in the practice of journalism, external goods that threaten to undermine the health of the practice, and virtues that sustain both the good work of individuals and the quality of the practice.

This concluding chapter will:

- Put online journalism in a different frame that connects with the previous discussion but highlights some key challenges for the future of the practice of journalism—challenges that relate to all four standards of excellence.

- Finish by looking at some qualities needed to do excellent journalism in this new world, the world of "both-and."

Table 8.1   Standards of Excellence in Online Journalism

Standard of excellence	Associated internal goods	Associated external goods	Associated virtues
Speed and accuracy with depth in breaking news	newness, knowledge, inquiry	status of being first, profit	initiative, perseverance
Comprehensiveness in content	knowledge, inquiry	profit; status from competition	initiative, perseverance, honesty, creativity, flexibility
Open-endedness in story development	knowledge, inquiry, discovery, fostering community, originality	status as journalists, profit	honesty, humility, perseverance, initiative, flexibility, creativity
Centrality of conversation	fostering community, knowledge, inquiry	profit	humility, honesty, courage

❖ THE WORLD OF BOTH-AND

It is dangerous to predict exact developments at a time when journalism and the environment in which it operates are rapidly changing. But what is virtually certain is that pursuing excellence in online journalism will involve living with several double-sided realities. These realities encompass how journalists think about their role and the role of the public, the forms and technological devices they use to present information, the sizes of the organizations in which they work, and how those organizations pay for excellent work. Together, these realities make the world of journalism a both-and, not an either-or, world.

A Critical Journalistic Eye and Respect for Citizen Contributions

The best of journalistic tradition puts reporters and editors in the role of skeptic (though not cynic) whether they are covering government, business, or other institutions. That watchdog role serves the public by helping to identify or prevent wrongdoing and questionable practices. Bill Kovach and Tom Rosenstiel, writing about the fundamental principles of journalism, stated the watchdog role this way: "Journalists must serve as an independent monitor of power" (2007, p. 140). They noted that this monitoring role encompasses not only government but "all the powerful institutions in society" (p. 142).

Journalists who are skeptical of the role of citizens in coverage may fear the loss of a critical role for themselves. But excellence in online journalism is wrapped up in not only the editorial judgment of journalists but also the questions raised by critical citizens and the knowledge they provide from their own worlds of work or home life. The discussion of open-endedness in story development in Chapter 5 made a similar point: that journalists need to look critically at user contributions while also respecting the public. More broadly, journalists need to continue doing their own independent reporting while communicating actively with readers and welcoming their insights. Learning how to do excellent work encompassing both traditional journalistic reporting and public knowledge has gone beyond important to unavoidable as more and more channels of communication with the public—for example, social media sites such as Facebook and Twitter—have sprung up. Many citizens use these channels to communicate directly with one another and bypass journalists. But social media create the potential to make conversation between citizens and journalists an even more central element of the practice.

Contributions from the public enable more information to get out quickly when numerous people report information instead of a single reporter running it down on his or her own. Journalists may be increasingly challenged to maintain both speed and accuracy because of the need both to work with citizen contributions—monitoring and responding to them—and to do independent reporting on important angles of a story. But media scholar Alfred Hermida argues that journalists also could play a role in developing tools to analyze and harness the ever-present wash of information from Twitter or related services in the future (Hermida, 2010). This kind of creative development and application of technology to help make sense of the constant flow of public communication might help to nudge the practice of journalism forward into another phase of understanding of excellence.

Pressure for profit, particularly in an uncertain economic climate, may still squeeze journalists for business reasons to rely more on content from the public and may make it difficult to find time to critically assess what citizens are saying. And it will always be a concern that few citizens will care about a story—or that those who get engaged helping to report or reacting will not reflect the breadth of the people it actually affects. It will always be difficult to foster conversation about issues as broadly or deeply as might be best to support the democratic purpose of journalism.

Complex and Simple Communication Forms on Big and Small Devices

As Chapter 4 discussed, being comprehensive in online coverage means making the most of the available media forms, picking the best ones for the story and the best mix of them. Those forms have developed in a way that they present a huge range of possibilities for communication. On one hand, designers can create intricate interactive graphics integrating databases and allowing exploration of a topic in multiple layers. On the other hand, text-based communication forms have developed that are more like headlines than stories. Text messaging and Twitter-style feeds can communicate stories or pieces of stories in a few characters. The development of these forms challenges online journalists to make the most of very different modes of storytelling. Wrapped up with the challenges of storytelling with this range of tools is the fact that different users see stories, or different chunks of stories, on devices ranging from huge monitors to tiny handheld screens.

Being comprehensive online looks more and more difficult as the forms and delivery vehicles multiply. It is unrealistic to think that, lacking unlimited time and money, journalists will be able to span the full range of storytelling possibilities on every major story and create the optimal mix. But it is increasingly important for journalists to think about the options in a way that makes judicious use of multiple forms. They must learn when it serves users best to focus on, for example, quick hits of text versus a blend of longer story and video. They must consider whether an intricate graphic will be too hard to see and navigate easily on a device like an iPhone. Working with so many possibilities takes flexibility and creativity, and often it will mean drawing on the best thinking and skills of others, not going it alone.

Big and Small Organizations as Places Where Excellent Work Develops

An assumption going into the research for this book was that big online news organizations would have more resources in staffing, time, and money. That is generally true and will probably continue to be even as the economic health of the established media industry remains uncertain. But amid the uncertainty in big media, small organizations have sprung up with enterprising individuals (such as Bob Gough at QuincyNews.org and Tracy Record at West Seattle Blog, discussed in Chapter 7) who have a passion for journalism and a desire to try it in new settings. Throughout the interviews, the desire for excellent work at some big organizations was evident. But the passion to do watchdog work locally and thorough community coverage at these small operations with limited resources offered new reason to be optimistic about the future of journalism.

Both large and small online news operations face considerable challenges in their pursuit of excellence. The journalists whose comments appear in Chapters 3 through 6 made it clear that time and staffing limits, along with competitive pressures, constrain them in their ability to present news quickly, accurately, and comprehensively. But at small operations such as those examined in Chapter 7, time and staffing pressures can hit home even more strongly. It is particularly hard for a small team of online journalists or an individual to be both fast and accurate and to go deep or use many presentation forms. When it comes to citizen contributions to story development and conversation, the small organizations can develop an advantage thanks to their close relationships with their readers. But finding the time to critically evaluate those comments or interact is difficult.

As for competition, small startups or sites based in long-standing community media may have an edge over big outlets in their areas if they have close relationships with their readers and focus more fully on intensely local coverage. But they occupy a vulnerable position. One of the greatest challenges for small sites trying to make money is whether they can make enough of it for continuing survival—not whether they are making too much of it and distorting their priorities.

For-Profit and Nonprofit Business Models

Chapter 7 looked at some of the kinds of media organizations, old and new, that have staked out territory online. News operations connected with newspapers or broadcast outlets of various sizes coexist with online-only ventures run by journalists from traditional news organizations, other citizens, or both. Models for financing these operations encompass a range including advertising to make a profit, as well as donations from philanthropic organizations or individuals. In the past, in the United States, nonprofit models were mostly limited to public television and radio. But recently, local and national web operations such as ProPublica offering investigative or special-topics coverage have added themselves to the mix. At the same time, as noted earlier, small for-profit operations have developed alongside the big mainstream outlets.

The challenges that for-profit operations face have been discussed throughout this book, including this chapter. But nonprofit models pose difficulties of their own. The benefit of freedom from profit pressures and from the potential influence of advertisers can lay a foundation for more aggressive investigative journalism and strengthen the watchdog monitoring of government and business. Consequently, nonprofit initiatives have a potentially important place in the continued health and development of the practice of journalism. But all pressures on excellence do not disappear. Funders may have political perspectives of their own that they state or imply they want represented. Major donors' contributions may fluctuate in value, leaving staffing levels to fluctuate as well. Donations from the broader audience may shrink in hard economic times and prove inadequate to support in-depth work.[1]

A broader array of media models, though, increases the likelihood that excellence in journalism will have the chance to continue evolving because pursuit of excellence will not depend primarily on a single type of financial support.

❖ WHAT IT TAKES TO WORK
IN THE WORLD OF BOTH-AND

Students entering the world of both-and, as well as journalists from old media adapting to it, will need skill sets that encompass multiple forms

---

[1]For a discussion of ethical issues associated with nonprofit investigative journalism, see Ward & Swanberg (2010).

of media and various shapes and sizes of communication devices. But doing excellent journalism in this environment takes much more than nuts-and-bolts skills. Less tangible qualities of character and habit—virtues—are necessary to think and act in a way that works to fulfill the journalistic *telos* of helping citizens "know well in the public sphere" (Borden, 2007, p. 50).

- Initiative and creativity drive journalists to think through how best to tell stories using both their own material and citizens' and to search out ways to present this material on different devices in various complex and simple media forms. These virtues are vital to maintain excellence when there is little time or staff to do a story—or skill sets are lacking among the journalists who are available.

- It takes flexibility to adapt to an environment of duality and rapid change. Flexibility is vital to work with different business models in organizations that may start, die, or change size quickly. It is also necessary to manage public contributions with both appropriate editorial judgment and openness to new voices, opinions, and angles for reporting.

- Perseverance enables journalists to pursue the most comprehensive coverage possible and to maintain a high standard of accuracy while living with expectations of quick reporting and the buildout of elements as a story develops. This is a virtue essential to the survival of strong investigative reporting that exposes problems in government and across society. Journalists have always had to dig deep to uncover important stories, but that becomes even more difficult when they have to juggle the expectations of multiple storytelling formats and multiplied deadlines.

- Humility is necessary to welcome and take seriously contributions from citizens who may not be trained as journalists but may have valuable information or leads to information, as well as opinions to offer.

- Honesty is needed to be clear with the audience about what information comes from where and to be transparent in conversation with users.

- It takes courage to allow robust conversation among users but also to rein it in when it becomes abusive.

In the challenging environment of online journalism, virtues are at least as important to good ethics and good work as the rules of ethics codes or company policies. Commitment to high standards needs to be deeply rooted in people, not just directed by outside pressure. Sandra Borden (2007), whose work entered the discussion throughout this book, pointed out that it is important not only for individual journalists to cultivate and practice virtues but also for those who care about the practice to consider how virtues help to sustain the practice itself. Much of the focus in this book has been on the ways individual journalists think about and contribute to standards of excellence. But more broadly, exercise of virtues helps to maintain the health of journalism and its ability to fulfill its *telos.* Examining and learning from the voices, virtues, and work of journalists who prize excellence is vital to sustain the practice of journalism and cultivate excellence in the field, in whatever forms journalism appears in the future.

❖ REFERENCES

Borden, S. L. (2007). *Journalism as practice: MacIntyre, virtue ethics and the press.* Burlington, VT: Ashgate.

Hermida, A. (2010, March 11). Twittering the news: The emergence of ambient journalism. *Journalism Practice.* [Early publication online].

Kovach, B., & Rosenstiel, T. (2007). *The elements of journalism: What newspeople should know and the public should expect* (Rev. ed.). New York: Three Rivers Press.

Lambeth, E. B. (1992). *Committed journalism: An ethic for the profession* (2nd ed.). Bloomington: Indiana University Press.

MacIntyre, A. (2007). *After virtue* (3rd ed.). Notre Dame, IN: University of Notre Dame Press.

Ward, S. J. A., & Swanberg, W. (Eds.). (2010, April). *Ethics for the new investigative newsroom: A roundtable report on best practices for nonprofit journalism.* Madison, WI: Center for Journalism Ethics. Retrieved May 27, 2010, from http://www.journalismethics.info/

❖ COMPANION WEBSITE

Visit the companion website at **www.sagepub.com/craigstudy** for links to examples of online journalism.

Index

About the Author

David A. Craig is a professor and associate dean for academic affairs in the Gaylord College of Journalism and Mass Communication at the University of Oklahoma. He teaches journalism ethics, editing, and graduate research courses. His research interests include excellence in journalistic practice in new and old media, the ethics of journalistic language, coverage of ethics in professions, and values for ethical decision making. Craig worked for nine years as a news copy editor. He earned an M.A. in communication from Wheaton College and a Ph.D. in journalism from the University of Missouri–Columbia. He taught editing courses at Northwestern University and Missouri. He has been a professor at Oklahoma since 1996.

Supporting researchers for more than 40 years

Research methods have always been at the core of SAGE's publishing program. Founder Sara Miller McCune published SAGE's first methods book, *Public Policy Evaluation*, in 1970. Soon after, she launched the *Quantitative Applications in the Social Sciences* series—affectionately known as the "little green books."

Always at the forefront of developing and supporting new approaches in methods, SAGE published early groundbreaking texts and journals in the fields of qualitative methods and evaluation.

Today, more than 40 years and two million little green books later, SAGE continues to push the boundaries with a growing list of more than 1,200 research methods books, journals, and reference works across the social, behavioral, and health sciences. Its imprints—Pine Forge Press, home of innovative textbooks in sociology, and Corwin, publisher of PreK–12 resources for teachers and administrators—broaden SAGE's range of offerings in methods. SAGE further extended its impact in 2008 when it acquired CQ Press and its best-selling and highly respected political science research methods list.

From qualitative, quantitative, and mixed methods to evaluation, SAGE is the essential resource for academics and practitioners looking for the latest methods by leading scholars.

For more information, visit **www.sagepub.com**.